DEEPEST
THANKS
DEEPER
APOLOGIES

Sunrise on the Tetons, 36″ x 48″

DEEPEST THANKS
DEEPER APOLOGIES

Reconciling Deeply Held Faith
with Honest Doubt

STEPHEN SHORTRIDGE

WORTHY
PUBLISHING

I dedicate this book with love to you, Cath, my best
friend, lover, and muse—and now, first editor.
You are a very busy girl.
I thank you, and I thank God for you.

*God has given everyone the freedom
of choice and the ability to create.
This book is about the times I have chosen God,
or chosen myself.
All our thoughts, words, and actions are the seeds we sow.
Our free will is a blessing or a curse. We decide.
Our choices are decisions to create life or death.
I ask you:
What will you create? Who will you choose?*

—S.C.S.

Private Garden, 24″ x 12″

CONTENTS

Amber Lit Solitude, 24″ x 30″

A NOTE OF EXPLANATION . . .

I paint with an impressionist style.

It's loose, and the broken brushwork is easily seen.

It's not finely finished, and a great deal of information is missing, requiring the viewer to fill in and participate.

I write like I paint.

I defend my writing style with words attributed to British journalist Malcolm Muggeridge: "Only mystics, clowns, and artists, in my experience, speak the truth, which, as [poet and mystic William] Blake keeps insisting is perceptible to the imagination rather than the mind. Our knowledge of Jesus Christ is far too serious a business to be left to theologians and exegetes alone."

I am not a theologian or an exegete. I am an artist by trade, a clown by default, a mystic by conviction.

All three are misunderstood, but none more so than the mystic. I use the term simply, as the saints of old did when a mystic believed there was a holy mystery to God.

We might say that a mystic believes we are God's works of art, and that God creates His art with an impressionistic style . . . that His loose and broken brushwork is easily seen throughout His creation . . . that His creation is not finely finished . . . that as He creates, a great deal of information is missing, creating mystery that requires deep faith to believe and deeper trust to obey.

And despite that deep faith and trust, honest doubt trickles in.

Reconciling honest doubt with deeply held faith is a paradox, something that seems unlikely, if not impossible, but turns out to be true. God makes it true. Paradox and contradiction are materials on His palette, along with consequence and conviction, all just as beautiful as the other colors He freely uses, like love and forgiveness. All to display His splendor.

I live my life in paradox immersed in mystery.

If I don't accept God's hand at work in the contradictions I experience, they're not mystery; they're just misery. In the midst of contradiction, I may be tempted to not trust God, but yielding to such temptation would throw me into the deception of trusting myself, whom I know better.

Sure, uncertainty is uncomfortable, at best, but I suggest avoiding people who claim the ability to "clearly" explain the mysteries of God. They've clearly not met Him.

What's on *Your* Palette?

While I see God as an impressionist, I see humanity, especially moral humanity, as more realist than impressionist. We all quote scriptures reflecting that God's ways are not man's ways, but because of sin we rebel against that truth. We want our way, not God's way. We want realism without contradiction, where everything is understandable without mystery or confusion.

Man's realism uses a self-made palette of doctrine, dogma, and self-righteousness to create human versions of judgment, condemnation, and lovelessness. In contrast, God's impressionism uses canvases of trials, uncertainty, and mystery to create His masterpiece of love, forgiveness, and mercy.

In my life of faith, I prefer impressionism to realism, trusting God in mystery rather than my own understanding. That preference puts me at odds with those Christians today who seem to imagine there are no mysteries about God. Which is quite a mystery, at least to me.

The beauty of being confused is that it allows me to find God's love in paradox, something that is true even though it may contradict belief and experience. The beauty of contradiction is His forgiveness in my uncertainty. This impressionism of God makes more sense to me as a mystery, and I agree with G. K. Chesterton's opinion that "mystery is the plainest part."[1]

Please understand that as I write, I don't imagine myself as Moses hurling tablets down on the children of Israel. Instead, I imagine that if you were to find me in that scene, I would probably be the artist working on the golden calf.

The mystery that God loves me, and any of us for that matter, is a profound one that I would rather receive than be required to understand.

The only paradox we like is one that suits us, not one that confuses us.

For many of us, mystery in our Christian experience was unwanted, and paradox was denied. As a result, much of our faith is based on our limited understanding and our hope in experiences rather than in God.

In life, when those "gods of experience" eventually fail us, our only choices seem to be a denying fantasy or a broken repentance.

But what we don't realize, or appreciate, is that it's in this very paradox of personal failure and in the mysteries of uncertainty that our faith matures and our need for God's love and forgiveness is made complete.

The most humbling of realities is also the most haunting of mysteries . . . that God loves us, forgives us, and desires a relationship with us, even when we wouldn't offer those things to ourselves. Especially when, despite our faith, we experience doubt.

Faith can thrive, naïve and ignorant, but faith that thrives in knowledge, after experience, has weathered the storms of doubt and confusion. My honest doubt has not been an enemy of God. God has used it to humble me.

God Wants to Love You

My prayers are not eloquent as much as heartfelt. I pray for you, and I pray for myself because life is full of beauty and images distorted with bad that looks good and good that looks bad. How can we know the truth when sometimes we feel deceived, and then we deceive ourselves by partnering in crimes against the One who loves us most?

As you age, I pray you gain more wisdom than I have. As I age, I am gaining the wisdom that too many of my hopes and desires have been selfish and self-serving.

I pray that God blesses you. I pray that He uses this book to bless you in spite of my efforts to be clever, in spite of my insecurity about being vulnerable, in spite of my fears to be fully known.

Are you sure you still want me to pray?

What can I hope and pray for you? For myself? For all those I love so dearly and for those I have harmed so deeply?

I pray that God blesses you to see His glory, and the glory from which you and I have fallen. I pray that God blesses you to see your need for His forgiveness, and to see your pride as His enemy. I pray you see and feel the love of Jesus Christ and that you love others as you repent of your selfishness. I pray you give God your shame and guilt, making room in your life for His abundant love, becoming a great storehouse of His love and forgiveness, filling it full, and then freely giving it away.

Finally, when mystery or experience confuses you, I pray that you trust when you cannot see, believe when you cannot understand, and love as God does when it seems you can't. God wants to love you. I pray you let Him.

God bless you. Amen.

Road Home, 36″ x 36″

INTRODUCTION:
THE COLORS ON GOD'S PALETTE

*Being unable to cure death, wretchedness, and ignorance, men
have decided, in order to be happy, not to think of such things.*

—Blaise Pascal, Pensees

The heights of beauty and the depths of depravity live on my block, sleep in my bed, wear my socks.

This is surely heaven, I tell myself when I look up at all the beauty. But then I look down at all the ugliness and say, *This is surely hell.* The sight of one fills me with hope. The sight of the other fills me with despair.

I am confused when hope and despair seem to appear on the same coin, and I'm equally confused when I sadly find a black desire in my own selfish flesh to not create beauty.

In my personal writings I've expressed my wonder about what beauty doesn't exist because we didn't create it. In this book I want to look at what I have already created, what I do create, and what I hope to create. As you read, I hope you will consider your creations as well—past, present, and future.

We are invited into this work by God, the impressionist Creator who left much of His creation unfinished. I believe He invites us to partner with Him by using the beautiful colors of His palette, not by scribbling over it with the drab charcoal in our pockets.

Testing Faith, Tasting Mercy

I've had my fifteen minutes of fame, as a twenty-something teen idol. I've lived in Manhattan and seen more of the world than most. But regardless of where I've lived, traveled, or worked, I've seen man blessed and cursed with the same beauty and the same destructive sin. Including myself.

Now that I am approaching sixty, I'm too old for a respectable mid-life crisis. I'll have to settle for an end-life crisis instead, with all its new revelations, temptations, and new challenges. If my age has let me acquire any wisdom at all, it is a better grasp of my own foolishness, along with the hope "that I have come to misunderstand a little less completely," as C. S. Lewis wrote.[1]

My life continues, part of it inexplicably ugly and part of it unexpectedly beautiful, forcing my joy and sorrow into a reluctant friendship. I lost my dad two years ago. Now, after all these months, my grief still wanders about without a home and surprises me like glimpses of beauty.

But as much as things appear to change, some stay the same; I still feel a dull fear that I'm being seduced by the world and betrayed by my religion. That my religion has not always served me in truth and in spirit.

It's my own fault. When I didn't like the way life was going, I created a faith using only the parts of the Bible I liked. I created a god that looked like me and then found fellowships that would accept my versions of God. No surprise, I failed at being my kind of "holy."

Maybe, like me, you too have failed. Perhaps you have been confused by yourself and the world you live in, and you still long for a relationship with our loving God who forgives us, understanding that we do not understand. *Deepest Thanks, Deeper Apologies* comes from a deep desire to strengthen that relationship, not by explaining the mystery of God or by removing all doubt, but to encourage mystery and raise doubt while reconciling those apparent uncertainties to our deeply held faith.

God's mystery surrounds me and always has. It surrounds all my experiences, all the people I've known and even the impostors I've been. But the greatest mystery in my life has been the undeserved grace of a loving God.

It's been easier to accept mysteries of God than to understand the mysteries of my own conflicted heart. Knowing God, sin seems insane; but knowing myself, it's not irrational. I continue to test faith and taste mercy, whole meals of it, while sometimes falling into doubt.

Amazingly, after a lifetime of forgiveness, He still calls me Beloved. How He can do this is part of the mystery—and my most practical doubt.

My hope is that in these pages you will come to believe that everything is spiritual and that we are all in a spiritual conflict where a large part is left a mystery. I think Pierre Teilhard de Chardin expressed our conflict best when he said, "We are not human beings having a spiritual experience . . . we are spiritual beings having a human experience."[2]

As spiritual beings, we accept that there is no *deepest* of God, only a *deeper*. My goal is to experience God's deeper and ever deeper revelations of His holiness and the unknowable depths of His love and forgiveness to me.

Deepest Thanks, Deeper Apologies is the difference between who I am and who I am becoming, as well as who I'm not and possibly never will be. Gratitude (deepest thanks) and regret (deeper apologies) measure the distance between who I am now and who I will one day be.

The Four Stages of Love

In my life, interesting ideas and artistic phrases sometimes come into my mind as unexpected impressions, perhaps only loosely related to what I am doing or saying or even thinking at that moment. Often they make me pause and think, or smile. I write them down—in my heart if not on paper. In these pages I share them with you the same way they occur to me, haphazardly, perhaps, and sometimes unexpectedly, with the hope that they make you think or nod or smile too.

They appear as lines of larger script, set into the page, or as a poem that falls wherever the thought landed in my writing. They come the way my brush comes to the canvas: more experienced than explained. Or, as the old Scot saying goes, "More felt, than 'telt.'"

They may seem out of place at first. But, as is true when viewing impressionistic art, you need to step back to see the picture, or, in this case, the premise, clearly. It's then that the individual colors and brushwork *do* come together. Working together, using contrast, they create a completed picture.

This "completed" book is divided into four sections based upon the "Four Stages of Love" described by Bernard of Clairvaux (1090–1153): Stage 1, I love myself for my sake; Stage 2, I love God for my sake; Stage 3, I love God for God's sake; and Stage 4, I love myself for God's sake.[3]

When I came across these stages, I was shocked at how accurate they were. I could look back on my life and see how I had tried to understand God, to use God, even to worship God for my own benefit. The stages display the mercy of God and His patience with us as we wander this road we call life.

They also display how, at the end of life—a place I think of as "where the road turns to water"—it will be God's faithfulness, not mine, that meets me. Amazing grace, isn't it?

Sum Total of Our Hungers

God promises us the desires of our heart. It's a dangerous promise when we don't have to choose God, for, as A. W. Tozer put it, "Every Christian will become at last what his desires have made him. We are all the sum total of our hungers."[4]

This book is about the times I have chosen God, or chosen myself. Who do *you* choose?

As I struggle to finish this project, I struggle in vain, because most things are never finished but are forever in process. And so, in my mind, the end of my book is punctuated not with a period but a comma. It ends not with a pronouncement but a plea. And the plea is this: Please. Consider the great responsibility you have. God has given you choices about who you will worship and what you will create.

We are all on this footpath of choices that leads to "where the road turns to water." Along that road you may see someone hungry, thirsty, or needing help. I hope you choose to stop. On any given day, it might be me lying there. On any other day, it might be you. Every day it will be Jesus.

Someday, we'll all see how our stories share in the larger story and were always somehow related. Until that day, my hope and prayer are that *this day* we all offer each other . . . "deepest thanks and deeper apologies."

Along for the Ride, 22″ x 16″

STAGE ONE

I Love Myself for My Sake

We begin with learned knowledge,
*   proud and filled with answers.*
We finish with learned ignorance,
*   humble and filled with awe.*
Do we become wise?
Or do we become tired of being fools?

—S.C.S.

Russian Children at Play, 48″ x 36″

THE JOURNEY BEGINS: BLINDED BY MY GLORY

I was driving on a hot summer's day . . . My only companions a
loud, frustrated life, a whining, disappointed self-righteousness,
and faith, riding silent in back. As I drove, the road turned to
water. I drove for hours and hours, chasing a mirage, but the water
always stayed just before me. I could see it, yet couldn't reach it.

I still haven't. Not yet.

—S.C.S.

Most of us start our adult lives hopelessly selfish, as selfish as
when we started our lives as children. But with the medications of
social constraint, or our fear of judgment in fellowship, we seem
to control it. Or is it just hiding?

In spite of all my efforts to outpace my selfishness, it always
catches up to me. It won't die. I've tried to kill it and have asked God
to kill it, but it remains. As long as I walk this road, it's the temptation that will accompany me, keeping pace with me as a constant

3

companion. Occasionally I feel victorious in my fight against it, and it seems to leave—but only to wait for a better opportunity to attack me when I'm weak, with only imagined strength.

My selfishness is a default position. When I don't choose to follow God, that choice defaults to my selfishness. Here, in stage one, without God, loving myself for my sake is a most reasonable action. It's programmed into me. Some people live their whole lives in this default mode, blinded by their own glorious selfishness, unable to see the glory of God that surrounds them.

But if we decide to follow God, our selfishness creates consequences, most of them bad. I am beginning to see that if I let my selfishness have its way, it leads me to a lonely kingdom, which is no kingdom at all. Just a king—me. And so our journeys begin, everyone selfishly deceived, everyone hopelessly proud.

Are We There Yet?

It's this self-centered mind-set that blinds us to misunderstand and soaks us with frustration on our journey. Even as adults we continue asking, like children, "Are we there yet?" And we are not.

How we deal with that truth is how we face this life and how we try to make things work. Everyone just wants to be happy, right? We try many things—including many things that harm us and others—and all the while we're still on this road, traveling.

This journey we share has a mystery that is not always enchanting and too often confusing. The uncertainties make it difficult. Some believe the road leads to nowhere. For me, it is a road to heaven, a road that stretches before me as it stretches my faith with doubt and questions my patience.

I wrote the poem "Where the Road Turns to Water" during a stretch of patience-testing road when I was feeling particularly frustrated; the promises of God felt like mirages, and my frustration led me to betray my truest longings. Blessed with exhaustion and mercifully wounded by futility, I could go no further.

Where the Road Turns to Water

Where the road turns to water,
The sun meets the sea . . .
Logic betrays, eyes deceive . . .
Only Love will prevail, only Love truly sees.

My best havings are but my wantings—
I reach forth with longing—
To where the road turns to water,
And the sun meets the sea.

Oh, to see, to taste, to feel, but sensing . . .
Mind and spirit outpaced—
The road blurs with water.
On knees knelt,
So drawn to remember . . . a place only felt.

See the sun meet the sea?
My rainbow's end,
Love waits for me.
Only Love will prevail, only Love truly sees . . .
Where the road turns to water.

Like a psalm, this poem was a plaintive plea for rescue. It was heard by a merciful God whose promises are true even if they are "not yet."

Where "the sun meets the sea" is where my Savior waits for me—not the mirage, but the reality. His love will prevail where the road turns to water.

What road are you on? Who's waiting for you where the road turns to water?

Authentic Contest

In painting, there must be a contest for the positions of mass and space. Everything is being challenged, pushed, and defined by the other. Where they meet, the apparent lines are energized by the contest. The vying, overlapping, and winning of their positions is unifying. Without this contest you have outlined objects, dismembered masses, and detached spaces.

In life, there is a contest for our souls. Everything I consider good or bad is being challenged, pushed, and defined by the other. The vying, overlapping, and winning of their positions is challenging and unifying. The honest struggle makes us authentic.

When I am not truthful about my struggles, my life is inauthentic. My life is dishonest. And in that life detached from reality, I build fortresses to defend my fantasies.

Anyone living in reality can see that I am not truthful. I am not just a bad witness; I am a fantasy witness. I am living amid fantasies that affect my faith by making God look like an escape from reality, instead of a way into it.

All along this road I travel, I see signs that seem to contradict each other. The distances and destinations are reversed. I'm surprised when I find the town of Foolishness is on the way to Wisdom, or that Pride is so close and Humility is so far away. This is paradox. It seems unlikely, if not impossible. But God makes it true.

Joys and Sorrows Share Tears

I find myself caught in the tension between what is and what could be while existing amid all the living out of the "not yet." In that tension, I struggle to make choices, and those choices have consequences that sometimes create contradictions.

I am sad to admit that, because of sin, I have never purely loved God or other people. I guess that would be both beautiful and sad, like seeing glimpses of heaven that somehow bring both bliss and torment, leaving me haunted by longing and full of regrets. Only by God's mercy have the redemption of those regrets and the fulfillment of those longings already begun.

It's here, under the same roof, that my joys of thanksgiving and sorrows of repentance share their tears and call me home. It's also here that I offer my deepest thanks to God and man for the beauty I see and experience. And I offer my deeper apologies for the times I have needed forgiveness.

The Swan Shepherd, 40″ x 30″

2

SELFISHLY DECEIVED
AND HOPELESSLY PROUD

Who would have guessed?
That in the knowing question of every three-year-old,
"Are we there yet?" lies the question
That haunts us all the days of our lives.

—*S.C.S.*

At the end of the movie *Tombstone,* as Doc Holliday is dying, he asks Wyatt Earp, "What did you want?"

Earp replies, "I just wanted a normal life."

Doc pauses then slowly answers, "There is no normal life, Wyatt. There's just life. Now get on with it."

There is no normal life. There is only normal sin, normal repentance, and holy redemption. Now get on with it. The only "normal" people are people we will never know. If we ever did *really* come to know them—they would stop being normal immediately.

When I think that others don't struggle in life, I'm just unaware. We all struggle on this road of life. There's no need to pretend. Our trials and struggles are alike in that they are unpredictable. They are unlike in that each of us struggles against something different. I should expect trials and be prepared for them. But predictably, when my sin creates a trial, I insist it's an accident. And once I am in a trial, I can be deceived, believing that all trials are evil; or despair, that trials cannot be turned to gold. When we choose sin and live our lives without God, why are we so shocked that trials turn into train wrecks? My efforts to deny or avoid life's struggles will only lead me to sin, because only sin promises me the world as I want it and not as it is.

Too often, because of my pride, I've refused God's help by denying my needs.

Believe me, my sin is no stranger to me. He looks and acts like an old friend, always happy to see me, wondering where I've been.

But in this stage of the journey, when I love myself for my sake, I don't seem to believe in sin or its consequence. I can't quite believe that this old friend would lie to me with the hope of destroying me. While I'm proudly reveling in my own successes, that attitude deceives me to assume my struggle is behind me. Or perhaps I acknowledge that trials are possible, but I try to anticipate when they will appear. I face the future as if I control it—or that it's out of control. Both are deceptions, and not trusting God in either, I fear.

Our struggles are real, and they are not then or there, but here and now. Not so much with others, but in the midst of ourselves.

Learned Ignorance

This spiritual life we are trying to learn may be as much about *un*learning as learning. We begin with learned knowledge, proud and filled with answers. But, hopefully, we end with "learned ignorance," as Nicholas of Cusa called it,[1] finishing with humility and filled with awe. Are you full of awe or full of yourself?

What we often consider wisdom is only experience. Do we really become wise, or are the wise tired fools?

As we begin our journeys, we still have too much unspent energy for our "self-love." Later, though, when we are finally spent, we grow tired.

We thirst . . . but not for God.

Not yet.

What if to know wisdom—I first need to know foolishness?
What if to find humility—I first need to know pride?
What if to find hope—I first need to know despair?
What if to find gratitude—I first need to know loss?
What if to find faith—I first need to know risk?

The Freedom of a Fool

What if to find wisdom—I first need to know foolishness?

Foolishness has been one of the ways I come to desire God's wisdom. It's not as if wisdom were lost; it's that I seem to do anything and go anywhere to avoid it. I think we keep foolishness in our lives because our sin calls it "freedom"—even though it is freedom from God. People imagine creative people are more passionate. Maybe they're just freer to have passions about God or something else.

My desire for wisdom was usually chosen by default, through defeat and, after the completed work of my foolishness, futility. The wisdom that can handle *this* kind of futility is the wisdom that has broken hope with anything but God himself. Because I love myself for my sake, that kind of wisdom is hard to find and comes at a great cost.

At this stage there are still so many choices and possibilities that I insist on trying. God may still be on my list of possibilities, but for now He's still near the bottom.

Much later I will come to realize that God's wisdom looks, sounds, smells, tastes, and feels a bit melancholy because it's linked to my sadness, the regret that His wisdom took so long to get and cost so much to gain. The cost was indeed great—to myself and to others, whether or not they know it.

Over the years, I have tried to gain knowledge about God and wisdom about myself, and in my quest I've been deceived by a godly hope: that knowledge and wisdom would result in obedience.

It does not. I still must choose to obey.

Futility can teach us wisdom, but only if it's wisdom that we want. King Solomon was thought to be the wisest man to ever live because as a young man he asked God for wisdom. But I was always confused about when he received it.

Was it the knowledge he was given about man and the universe that made him the wisest man? Or was it the later failure and desires of his own heart that made him the greatest fool? Or was it both?

What if God's gift of wisdom included a full knowledge of yourself? A knowing that revealed a rebellious heart in need of redemption? A knowing that revealed a complete understanding of foolishness *and* the complete knowing of your need as well?

In my personal experience, when I have gained wisdom, I have better understood it in terms of foolishness rather than theology.

Bouts of Arrogance and Near-fatal Pride

Humility is an experienced virtue. It usually comes from having survived bouts of arrogance and near-fatal pride. The truth is, someone who is greatly humble has been humbled greatly. Humility is not a badge of honor but a Purple Heart given to those wounded in battle who survived to tell their stories.

Pride comes before a fall, and a fall comes before a humbling. The higher the pride, the greater the fall. The greater the repentance, the greater the forgiveness. The greater the forgiveness, the greater the love. I have received much love.

A. W. Tozer reminds us that there are "two classes of Christians: the proud who imagine they are humble and the humble who are afraid they are proud. There should be another class: the self-forgetful who leave the whole thing in the hands of Christ and refuse to waste any time trying to make themselves good. They will reach the goal far ahead of the rest."[2]

When I imagine what the self-forgetful class might look like, I imagine it as preschoolers finger-painting with God, hands touching and paint on their faces, laughing.

Humility is an expression of childlike gratitude; pride, an expression of adult foolishness. Being an artist is a childlike endeavor that requires wonder to be successful. I watch grown-ups and feel especially grateful to God that I have not completely forfeited the playful wisdom of a child.

There have been times in my life when I was very adult. My life was busy; I was very important but rarely satisfied. I looked everywhere for answers, but I had no idea what I was looking for. These are the "adult" traits of pride.

Proudly Humble

When I didn't have the god I wanted, I made one. Of course, he was my God; everyone else made their own. In church one Sunday I had a vision of sorts. God showed me people worshiping different gods while He stood off to one side, very sad, as He watched these people worshiping their gods of health, of prosperity, spiritual gifts, and more. The childlike faith that pleases a holy God is not sophisticated enough for such mature deceptions.

Oh, but that deceptive pride is seductive. It calls my selfishness Beloved—*dearly* Beloved. And when I least expect it, I'm beguiled. I'm nearly defenseless against its wooing because we've been intimate friends my entire life. At this stage, I don't yet realize that I am being betrayed, that it is not my friend but my foe. And then comes my pride's greatest trick of all: the blinding deception of convincing me that I'm humble.

Now I realize that those rare times when I did feel humble were only preludes to my repentance. (Self-righteousness is not limited to the religious—all that's required is small amounts of humility and adequate pride.)

When you love yourself for yourself and not because you are God's creation, you believe you're complete in yourself. You need no one else. You don't need to impress anyone; you impress yourself. And now, feeling self-satisfied, you compliment yourself with thoughtful praise, "I'm so proud of how humble you've become."

Imagine—

Trying to weave a tapestry taken off the loom.

Nothing stays true.

It becomes difficult, and then impossible, as it tangles and knots,
    distorting the image,
        making the original design unrecognizable.

Without the parameter of the loom, the work is lost to itself,

And with no hope of being what it was, it becomes something else.

In the end

It is no tapestry at all, just a large ball of tangled yarn.

Complex, with beautiful knots, and lots of pretty colors to look at . . .
    but useless as a tapestry.

Much of this life is woven off the loom.

Especially the beautiful knots of man's philosophies,

"I must be God," said as statement, politely.

And eventually, the pretty colors,

"I will be God," said as a challenge, defiantly.

The Word Is *Who,* Not *What*

My wife's grandmother was a godly woman who lived and died in the dirt-poor hills of West Virginia. She lived the Scriptures. One day my wife, Cath, asked her dad, "Did Grandma read her Bible every day?"

He paused and then, through tears, said, "Oh, honey . . . she couldn't read."

You don't have to read to know the Word—but you can read the Word without knowing.

There are the misconceptions that knowledge is more important than experience and that experience is more important than truth. These misconceptions have settled into two camps of religion: one assumes knowledge creates a relationship with God; the other assumes experiences are evidence of that relationship.

Both, when taken to extremes, end up as lies, and those who hold them, failures. I've seen Christians who could preach the knowledge that God is love without loving, and I've seen others reject seekers who didn't share their same experiences of the "love" of God. Such twisted thoughts amaze me because 1 Corinthians 13 states the truth so clearly, listing all the good things we can do and get from God. And then God finishes the list with the warning that they're *all* worthless if they're done without love.

Knowledge and experience are important, and paradox can be confusing, but here's the truth: the unloving contradiction of a Christian is always sin.

Give Me What I Want

Pride and selfishness eventually lead to the misconceptions linked to knowledge and experience, and then to failure. But even when we think we're on our last hope, it rarely is. It's often just the last hope *before* the last hope, which is no hope at all but simply an ultimatum to God: "Give me what I want!"

Now, if I really used my last hope for what I wanted, instead of for God—and didn't get it—that's where my faith would get tested. And for me, that would usually happen when I thought I deserved a blessing.

Too often, when we don't get our way, we break off our relationship with God, and as a consequence we feel as if all hope, faith, and love disappear. Then, after the free fall of doubt and apparent betrayal, our tested faith is revealed for what it is: a greater faith and trust in God, or else a fading memory of something that never existed.

Depending on the consequences of my actions, I may want to believe in fate or predestination. And though I believe in God's predestination—for me—predestination is the certainty that I must make choices. Not that I already have.

Until God is my *only* hope, I may hope in anything but God, including a Christianlike god. A god of my choosing is essentially a god of my making, one that I can pick out, as I might choose a car for its features: I like this model, this doctrine, and I'll take that upgrade with the gifts of the Spirit.

Aristotle said, "It is the nature of desire not to be satisfied." I agree, and I imagine the holy discontent I have is positive evidence of its truth. However, there are negatives in desire. In fact, we all probably fear our passions on some level. If not, we should. Our desires and passions are God's design; they're for our good.

Our problems arise when we pervert our desires or place them above God. C. S. Lewis reminded us, "You can't get second things by putting them first; you can get second things only by putting first things first."[3] Everything must become second to God. *Everything.*

The "god" in the Mirror

One evening at a men's growth seminar at Church On The Way in California, Pastor Jack Hayford told us that when he got out of bed every morning, he didn't land on his feet but on his knees. He made sure he started each day seeking the reality of who he was and who God was, establishing the relationship of a holy God and a forgiven saint.

I don't know who said this, but I agree: "Every morning I wake an atheist." Every morning, I must decide to worship God, or not. I don't hit my knees every morning, but I should—because danger is waiting not far from my bed. The danger being that reality may become fantasy by the time I reach the bathroom mirror, where, preening through my folded face, instead of worshiping a holy God, I begin my blurry worship of the god in the mirror.

God is missing in this reflection. I only have eyes for me.

The Gates, Central Park, NYC, 48″ x 36″

IMAGINING OUR STRENGTH
AND OTHERS' WEAKNESS

With money, power, or fame, you might be able to handle one
"Thank You, God."
With two, your chances diminish: "God who?"
With all three, you're lost: "I'm God."

—S.C.S.

Many imagine they could handle money, power, or fame—but they're mostly dressed-up soldiers nowhere near the front. Watching where others have failed, they imagine their own strength. And having never been really tempted or tested, they claim victory in a battle of a war that never took place.

Too much wealth, fame, or power can create a form of delusion. Our material gains should reveal our spiritual needs. But if that doesn't happen, a distance grows between the two, and in this expanding void, flames of delusion ignite. We lose sight of our deepest longings and settle for everything else.

It is God alone who comes to rescue us from that place. We all seem to find Him by running into Him as we leave the burning building and the fire we started. The first thing we do is thank Him by becoming pious; the second, with our hair still smoking, is to imagine our strength and others' weakness. Our first thank you, imagining our holiness, and the second, imagining someone else's unholiness. Both views are distorted by the lingering haze of self-conceit.

Refining Pride

When people take joy in the failures of others, I wonder: is it the only place to find comfort for their own? We watch lives at a distance and imagine all kinds of wonderful and horrible things. We have no idea what others have faced or are facing, or what hopes and fears they have for tomorrow.

Plato reminded us to "be kind, for everyone you meet is fighting a great battle."[1] And Jesus reminds us to love . . . even our enemies.[2]

Which raises a question. My spiritual journey begins, and the first skill I acquire is that of judging others. Why do I do that? Why do I judge?

Because loving myself for my sake has made me proud, not humble.

With the help of my pride, I begin refining my self-righteousness by imagining my greater spiritual strength and imagining others' greater weaknesses.

The Bible encourages us to not grow "weary in well doing" as we assist those who are weaker.[3] But I imagine the weariness is not struggling with others' weaknesses, as much as it is struggling with our own.

Paul's inspired encouragement to the Galatians also speaks directly to me, encouraging and inspiring me to persevere in these struggles:

> Steve, live creatively, as a friend. If you see others fall in sin, help them. And if need be, forgive them, and save your criticism for yourself. Did you forget? I will judge you as you judge others. Besides, it's early. Trust Me, you may need forgiveness before the day's out. Help those who are oppressed and get your hands dirty with good work. Share the burdens of others and you will complete my law with love. If you think you're too good for that, you're not thinking right.[4]

I'm Not Alone in Here

When I was told that schizophrenics are often preoccupied with religion, my first thought was, *Which one* and, *Which one?* After amusing myself with what I had just written, I thought about it. It would seem obvious that, in those who are divided, the division would probably include divisions between what they considered right and wrong or between what they consider good and evil. Surely somebody in their group would try to find God, knowing everyone else in the group is so messed up. The dilemma for me as a "normal" person, without being schizophrenic, is living with all these people and not dividing them.

When you love yourself for your sake, there is a surprising

wholeness about your life. You are completely and hopelessly selfish, your pride fully dictates, and you are unreservedly dominated by your desires. The commitment to yourself is "all in."

But then there appears a rebel in the camp, a covert conspirator that ruins the fun of it all.

At first I imagined this spoiler as evil, but in the end it was good—in fact, the only Good. The blessing was confusing because I was in conflict with myself. I realized for the first time that a real battle was taking place inside me as I made decisions to be selfish or to be loving. And I couldn't understand *why* I wanted to be more loving.

I understand now that I am not alone in here; I have at least a good and bad twin living inside me. Selfishness offers me a counterfeit completeness. Only God alone, as I allow Him, is capable of redeeming me, whole and holy, one healthy consistent personality throughout.

The Stuff of Religion

Jesus said, "In this life you will have tribulation." There are some things in the Bible that are hard to understand, and there are things we do understand but pretend we don't. John 16:33 is neither.

I found a T-shirt—a funny, vulgar T-shirt about modern-day "tribulation"— being sold on the streets of Lower Manhattan. It clearly explained the world's religions, which is quite a feat for a T-shirt. I rewrote it to clean up the vulgarity and added some conclusions of my own:

In this life I will have "Stuff." What can I do with my Stuff? I need religion for my Stuff . . .

Taoism: Stuff happens.

Hinduism: This Stuff has happened before.

Confucianism: Confucius say, "Stuff happens."

Buddhism: It is only an illusion of Stuff happening.

Zen: What is the sound of Stuff happening?

Islam: If Stuff happens, it is the will of Allah.

Atheism: Stuff evolves randomly.

Agnosticism: Maybe Stuff happens and maybe it doesn't.

Jehovah's Witnesses: Knock, knock . . . Stuff happens.

Protestantism: Stuff won't happen if I work harder.

Catholicism: If Stuff happens, I deserve it.

Judaism: Why does this Stuff always happen to me?

After all the religions—I still have my Stuff. Who will deliver me from my Stuff?

Jesusism: All who are weary, give me your Stuff.

Life Is a Puzzle

Have you ever done a puzzle and found, as I have, that some pieces fit where they didn't belong?

They're the right color and shape, they appear to fit, and I *want* them to fit because that would bring the puzzle closer to completion. But if I misplace the pieces, the puzzle is confused and impossible to finish. Later, I finally understand when I find the errant pieces. Now I really can move ahead and finish the puzzle. I should be relieved.

When I was younger and bumping about in this stage of "selfish-being," I searched for the answers to life in religion and philosophy. I imagined that I just hadn't met the right people, found the right books, or had the right teachers to complete this puzzle. For years, I thought I was only lacking information to make sense of this life.

Now I find religion making the same mistake. Still trying to make that piece fit. Until the relationship-with-God piece is put in its proper place, I will face my life's puzzle with confusion and find it impossible to finish.

No one would wish to be blind.
But when we willfully shut our eyes to God,
we needlessly stumble about as if blind,
and imagine a curse by refusing a blessing.

In religion, knowledge and relationship may appear to be similar in appearance, but they are different pieces of this puzzle. Trying to place knowledge where relationship belongs is what confused my puzzle. Confused, I try to fit the pieces of reason where faith belongs. Or I try to force understanding to fit where the mystery piece belongs.

The most important piece of this puzzle is my relationship with God—because without that relationship, none of my puzzle makes any sense at all.

Logic for Fantasies

As I look through a screen door, my view is barely hindered. Nonetheless, my view is patterned by it. What is the pattern on my screen: Selfishness? Unforgiveness? Self-righteousness? Kindness or love? How many screens are there? Do I interpret life through them? Of course I do. We all do, whether we want to or not. It's a puzzling mystery how my logic can betray and my eyes deceive. Just as there are mysteries about God, I find there are mysteries about me. I've come to realize, painfully, that my perspective is not always to be trusted, as I once thought it was, and that sometimes my logic is better suited for fantasy than for facing the real challenges in my life.

My perspective is a selfish thing. It's the only one I have without God's love. When I view life through the perspective of God's love, I can see as He does. And when my logic is based on God's truth, I'm surprised to find myself loving as He loves.

Our perspective about life is so important because we are dominated by it, and often inaccurately.

For an artist, the problem of perspective first starts with looking and not seeing. A new art student inevitably draws a swan with a neck that's too short and a beak that's too little. Or if not too little then a beak in the shape of a duck's, or a goose's, or a crane's. The beginning artist is looking without seeing.

Likewise, as I've learned, when you begin writing you soon realize you can't see your own mistakes. You lack experience and knowledge to work the craft because you haven't learned it yet. You need someone who has learned before you to be your teacher.

Most of the time, the same is true for spiritual perceptions. When we first start to look at God, we don't see Him rightly. In my case, Christ is *taller* than I first imagined, and His holiness *bigger* than I first thought. My perceptions were based on false assumptions rather than on the Word of God, the reality of God.

City lights, man-made stars, shrines of shining beauty. But unlike stars scattered in the night, they shine in rows bound to the glow, at the end of a pole, only bright enough to blind our view of eternity.

(I wrote this, considering how man's philosophies, even though they're not so bright, can still blind us to seeing God.)

We look but we don't really see. Sometimes because, conveniently, we don't want to.

Disciplines are what bring maturity, and in this comparison, accurate perceptions. The disciplines required for spiritual maturity are like most other things we attain ability for or accuracy about. From a teacher, an artist learns to draw, a writer learns punctuation. From the Master Carpenter, a Christian learns to create the life of Christ.

Blindness with Reason

There are times when I have felt uneasy while visiting Florida. At first I thought it was because there's nothing taller than the buildings. But what I've come to realize is that I actually feel claustrophobic. For me, without mountains and a wide-open vista, my view is limited to the press of my immediate surroundings. In Florida, I can see no farther than that house, that building, or that tree. My world becomes smaller, my vision shortsighted, my perspective limited. Claustrophobic.

Similarly, for faith, I need God's greater perspective, because evil presses and pushes the cares of this life into my view, not just blocking my view of reality and putting doubt in the way of my faith, but attacking my faith head-on by eliminating my view of God.

With a limited perspective I come to believe that what matters is only what I see. And if my view of God is completely blocked, I may come to believe there is no God at all. When people don't see God, I wonder if it's something like that.

Preferred Perspective

We have a preferred personal perspective. For instance, there's our perspective on justice. We expect fairness, *our* fairness; we expect that the just will prevail and that we are the just; the wicked will be punished, and we are *not* the wicked. (We tend to suffer from incurable short- and long-term memory loss.)

In the perception of ourselves, we miscast ourselves as the heroes and not the villains. We think too highly, or too fantastically, about ourselves. We imagine we are as righteous and innocent as Job, and we ignore the fact that we are his idiotic, unloving, and self-righteous friends.

I read about the children of Israel and imagine they were stiff-necked and ungrateful fools as they wandered, whining, through the desert while being graciously preserved by a patient (well, most of the time patient) God. But somehow, I don't recognize my own voice in their chorus of complaints.

I imagine my strength and judge the failures of others. I want to be David only when he kills Goliath, and not when he murders Bathsheba's husband and takes his wife.

I need fellowship, because I need people around me who know God, who know me, and who know when I'm being an idiot—and love me enough to tell me so.

My memories are selective, and I need God to answer who I am because only He truly knows. Only He can save me from my own delusions.

And then, when it comes to our religious perspectives, it's like closing one eye and looking through a roll of toilet paper. Our clarity chosen, our understanding limited, standing on tiptoes, we peer through our own telescopes and contest each other's toilet paper beliefs: debating the strength, ply, and softness.

Spiritual Fog

There is another altering perception that is evil; it is what I call "spiritual fog." Like a physical fog, spiritual fog doesn't change the reality of the "landscape" around me; it changes my perspective.

I have felt spiritual confusion, and it's more than imagination. It's real, and when it's evil, it can be as tangibly real as physically losing your balance. Only in this case, it attacks your spiritual equilibrium. The confusion can arrive through argument or situation, but when you sense spiritual fog, I hope you will realize immediately that you're under attack. When you feel it enveloping you, run, don't walk, to God.

For me, spiritual fog is blinding, and if it's thick enough, can create such vertigo that I no longer know up from down, or even right from wrong.

Physical dizziness takes us to our knees. The loss of spiritual equilibrium should do the same. And quickly.

The Wisdom of a Fool

On this journey I have finally come to God on my "me" list, and the timing is good because I have grown tired of being blind and a fool. The other day I heard someone say that he had "surrendered to God," but I imagined that wasn't the whole truth. The whole truth was probably that he had finally given up and simply *called* it surrender.

I begin this new faith motivated by my pride and a belief in "cosmic karma": the hope that doing enough good can outweigh all the bad I've created (something that, to present, I've tried unsuccessfully to do, but my pride still petitions for).

This life has not allowed me to neatly package it. It has been messy and more confusing than I first thought—or than I ever thought. The good and bad seem random, but I sense there's more to their occurrence. I just can't quite explain it—yet. To love myself for my sake has provided fewer answers and less satisfaction than I could have ever hoped or imagined.

This part of the journey hasn't been completely fruitless. My failures have limited my options. I've gained the wisdom of a fool, and now I know I need God.

After all the confusion and frustration, I realize—regardless of the unexplainable mysteries about God, or about myself—that my will is still mine to control and that my decisions are still mine to make. The good news/bad news is that my choices are becoming simpler, not more complex. I can either choose to please me . . . or to please God.

This road I've traveled has carved a big circle in some desert, leaving me where I started, standing at a crossroads. It's an intersection of many roads, but looking to the right, where the road disappears, I can see a distant reflection of water. And choosing the right road, I press on.

Finding Your Nose

After surviving this "I love myself for my sake" stage, I'm left with much that I don't understand, and what I do understand sometimes confuses me. I am surprised to find that the spiritual life does not solve mystery but merely introduces me to more mystery—a mysterious place, not where I find all my answers, but the place where I find God.

Brennan Manning quipped: "Blessed are the sensible, for they shall see the tip of their nose."[5] Now, I wouldn't argue for anyone to be "unsensible," but I do argue that if you *only* use your senses to make sense of this life, then when you run into paradox, contradiction, or mystery, you'll be lucky to find your nose.

Remember the Beatitudes, what I call God's Manifesto of Paradox:

You're blessed when you're at the end of your rope. With less of you there is more of God and his rule.

You're blessed when you feel you've lost what is most dear to you. Only then can you be embraced by the One most dear to you.

You're blessed when you're content with just who you are—no more, no less. That's the moment you find yourselves proud owners of everything that can't be bought.

You're blessed when you've worked up a good appetite for God. He's food and drink in the best meal you'll ever eat.

You're blessed when you care. At the moment of being "care-full," you find yourselves cared for.

You're blessed when you get your inside world— your mind and heart—put right. Then you can see God in the outside world.

You're blessed when you can show people how to cooperate instead of compete or fight. That's when you

discover who you really are, and your place in God's
family.

You're blessed when your commitment to God pro-
vokes persecution. The persecution drives you even
deeper into God's kingdom.

Not only that—count yourselves blessed every time
people put you down or throw you out or speak lies
about you to discredit me. What it means is that the
truth is too close for comfort and they are uncomfortable. You can be glad when that happens—give a cheer,
even!—for though they don't like it, I do! And all heaven
applauds. And know that you are in good company. My
prophets and witnesses have always gotten into this
kind of trouble.[6]

To desire those blessings spelled out in Matthew 5 instead of
what I desire is a lifetime battle. My desires are beginning to long
for God, but they will never be satisfied. To be satisfied is contrary
to God's design and, if attained, would have to be some form of
death. Life with God will be a growing revelation without end.

The Beatitudes seem puzzling to us, fragments of paradox.
But these pieces fit together to form a whole picture for Him. He
wants me to imagine life as whole and holy, to see *my* life as whole
and holy too. And yours.

The First Prayer

Our Father who art in heaven, hallowed be Your name.
God, if You're real, please help me. And if You're God, I'm sorry we haven't talked before.

Your kingdom come, Your will be done, on earth as it is in heaven.
God, it's not going well for me down here. If You would help, I could use some of Your heaven on my earth.

Give us today our daily bread.
I've made a mess of things, and I owe a lot of money. Please send money.

Forgive us our debts, as we also have forgiven our debtors.
You forgave me my mistakes. Thanks. But how can You expect me to forgive those sinners? I was told You see everything—don't You see what they've done to me?

And lead us not into temptation, but deliver us from the evil one.
I'm trying, I really am, but I have a hard time resisting what I know is wrong. And if You're my friend, I guess I have an enemy also, so I would appreciate anything You can do to help me with that. But please, please don't send me to Africa. And please don't make me be a monk. Thank You. Amen.

Venice Light, 24" x 48"

STAGE TWO

I Love God for My Sake

There are dangers in coming to religion
before coming to God.
We become proud instead of humble,
wise in our own eyes.
We imagine that changing the labels on our lives
is changing the content.
And we're deceived to think that
He loves us because we first loved Him
when it's the other way around.

—S.C.S.

Arriving at the Met, 12" x 24"

THE GOOD FORTUNE OF
A GOOD GOD TO HELP ME
ON MY JOURNEY

Aristotle said I am a rational animal; I say I am an angel
with an incredible capacity for beer.

—*Brennan Manning,* Ragamuffin Gospel

Nothing good or bad seems to happen all at once. Rather, good or bad, beauty or ugliness, proceeds from what we choose to hold on to or let go of and, as a result, what we gain and what we lose.

Experience should have taught us by now that what we touch touches us, what we embrace embraces us, and what we grab is where we are held. Paul said in Romans that if we use this freedom, this gift from God, to choose sin, it may be our last free act.

When I take hold of sin, sin takes hold of me. And later, sometimes much later, when I prefer to let go, sin still prefers to hold me in its grasp.

Wasted Miles

We choose the roads we're on. Free will is a blessing and a curse. My choices decide which.

If I left Los Angeles for New York, for example, would it matter if I went through Reno instead of Albuquerque, when my final destination was still New York? And why would I be so upset with someone who went through Seattle? We all take different routes, even to God. But if He is our final destination, then regardless of where we've gone or shouldn't have gone, when we arrive, He will have redeemed it all . . . all those wasted miles and all that wasted life.

It's relatively easy. We all can plot the shortest distances to New York and to God, but none of us, because of sin, have ever taken the short route.

We want to see the world and even revisit places we shouldn't. Free will is like a free pass that we can use anytime to go anywhere we choose. Consequently, we have all gone astray.

Until I surrender my free will to God, I will wander. And until I surrender my religion to God, I will believe He loves me more for taking a shorter route.

When life becomes difficult, I know I need something more to be successful. I need God for my sake. I have made such a mess of my life that I'm brought to my knees—almost. From where I sit, I call out to God, "I need You. I will give You my life." I imagine that God should be thrilled to know that I want Him. That's why I will still be deceived for now, because it's my selfishness that now loves God . . . for *my* sake.

What? God loves me? Good! He can help me get what I want in this life.

The Conspiracy of Me

In the beginning of my relationship with God, when I discover that God loves me and wants to forgive me, my first response is gratitude.

My second is a selfish hope.

Now, with a God to serve me, life will be better. I'll be happier. And my life will be full of blessings. Because God loves me.

When I came to the end of my bad . . .
I called Him Savior.

Of course I will decide *what* blessings. Just tell me what I need to do to give me what I want, and I'll do it.

This stage where I love God for my sake, may awaken me spiritually, but I am still selfishly confused. I do want to change, but my selfishness changes like a chameleon's—only in color, only on the surface. I am truly grateful to have God help me as I begin planning and creating my own heaven on earth. And the first thing I create is God in my own image.

I've heard the famous, and the otherwise, say at the end of their lives, "I have no regrets." I don't understand that and find it hard to believe. I have lots of regrets, and not just for my failures— the bad—but for my lost opportunities at good. There were too many to count, and they were too heavy to bear. So when Christ offered to take them, I gladly gave them. Mercifully, God forgives me for all I did—and for all I didn't.

But now that I'm forgiven, I'm confused. Why do I still struggle if I'm forgiven? At this point I imagined there would be little conflict, and what conflict I did face would be easily handled now that I have God on my side. He *is* on my side, right? So why is life so hard?

I sense a conspiracy.

I still have this group of old friends who conspire to keep me from living my life for God. I notice them lurking about, and I know them all by name: Pride, Lust, Sloth, Gluttony, Greed, Vanity, and Revenge.

I left no forwarding address, but somehow they have found me. I see them so frequently that I'm starting to think they've moved into the same neighborhood.

Reduced to Rule Keeping

In painting, I stay as loose as I can for as long as I can. Because defining too soon confines the creative process. The more I do it, the more limited the creative process becomes.

There is a parallel in religion. If, with my new knowledge, I give in to the temptation of defining too soon, that knowledge makes rules. Lots of rules. And my faith becomes not so much about God and what He does as much as it is about my ability to quantify and qualify my own sin. I end up only measuring what I do and measuring others for what they do. I become my own savior while I condemn others.

When my spiritual life is reduced to rule keeping, the process of growth slows and then stops. Paul, in Galatians 3, asked, "Did you receive the Spirit by the works of the law, or by believing what you heard? Are you so foolish? After beginning by means of the Spirit, are you now trying to finish by means of the flesh?"[1]

It was only the sin in my life that could think "a proud man of faith" is not an oxymoron. And, it was my failure to be holy that helped me understand I was just a moron.

Rules don't require faith; rules don't even need God. But rules give us real options to make ourselves into gods. Timothy Keller explains the process well: "There are two ways to be your own Savior and Lord. One is by breaking all the moral laws and setting your own course; and one is by keeping all the moral laws and being very, very good."[2]

"I still love you, Steve"

People who have all the answers have not been confused by experience. That's why it makes no sense to me that the parent of eight- and ten-year-olds would teach successful-parenting techniques. Most likely, it would only make them proud and upset others who have teenagers. When one's children are twenty-three and twenty-five, then that parent might have some parental wisdom.

By then he or she will surely have experienced parenting success *and* failure somewhere along the journey.

The leader I trust most has known, and knows, his or her sin and is a leader who also knows the deeper love and forgiveness of God. Without that experienced brokenness, there is a danger of great pride—and probably a great fall as well.

Years ago, there were times when my failure at rule keeping caused me to struggle greatly. It was a struggle to believe I was even saved. But then a day arrived when I finally understood the message in Romans 7:

> What I don't understand about myself is I decide one way and then do the other—do something I despise. I agree with You, Lord, and Your commands, but I can't seem to do them. This desire to sin trips me up even when I want to do what's right. I will to do good . . . but I don't do it. I decide to not do bad, and I do it anyway. I love You, Lord, and I delight in Your ways, but something has gone wrong. I betray even myself. And when I least expect it, sin rebels in me and takes over.
>
> Please, Lord, I need help. I seem to be losing the battle for me.
>
> Oh, wretched man that I am, who will save me from myself—and this life of sin?
>
> Jesus.[3]

I could again hear God speaking to me through these verses. I wept and heard the answer to my prayers: *I still love you, Steve.*

I Look Just Like Me

The "I love God for my sake" stage is proving to be of benefit, but this newfound faith of mine is being rocked by self-betrayal. My best efforts to be holy and live this life of faith are being sabotaged. What I'm most shocked to discover is that *I* am responsible for the destruction. My "self" is the saboteur. I would prefer to blame someone else for my failures, and whenever possible, I do. And I feel justified to do so because I feel so sincere about my desire to be good. If confronted, I will deny those are my fingerprints at the scene of the crime.

For now, even my efforts to be holy are for *my* benefit and *my* profit. My relationship with God is a serving one—serving me.

And though my selfishness has somewhat abated, it's still alive and well, lurking in the shadows. I know I still sin. At this stage, if I were honest, I'd admit that I often still like it, as long as I get a break on the consequence.

My Absurd Hope

I am now frustrated with God—or is it with my religion? I don't understand it; everyone else seems to be doing fine. I'm tired of this battle, but I'm learning it's easier to cover over my failures with religion rather than deal with them openly and honestly.

I can't let anyone know how I struggle and fail. I need a strategy. Did I pray? I must have because I got an answer: "Put more effort into your religious appearance."

My absurd hope is that if I look like a Christian and quack like a Christian . . . I will become a Christian duck. This logic, as it fails, requires more commitment to my self-righteous disguise and a louder quack. I hadn't noticed, but I'm sure others have. I've developed a very spiritually sophisticated and affected duck-like walk.

Addicted to Self-Righteousness

It seems the only addiction some people suffer is self-righteousness. So trying to explain bondage to someone who hasn't had the "experience" is like describing the colors of a sunset to the blind. It's true you may not understand; but worse, you may think you do.

Proverbs tells us to "above all else gain understanding," but then promptly warns us "not to lean on it." The reason? Understanding only provides the opportunity to choose. My understanding can choose lovelessness; my faith should not.

When we are in sin, we can either comfort ourselves with the deception that the worst sins are not ours or we can find comfort with God in repentance. With one we find comfort; with the other, comfort and forgiveness.

Maestro, 30″ x 24″

THE APPEARANCE OF EVIL—
OR GOOD

As to that which I am ignorant of concerning
myself, I remain ignorant of it until my darkness
shall be made as the noonday in your sight.

—Saint Augustine

When we see good behavior we think, *Good people . . . maybe.* But the real truth is, most murders occur in the heart and most adultery in the mind.

Too often, our goodness is lived out only in performing for each other. That performance may be only the *appearance* of evil or good. Spiritual clarity comes when I get alone with God. It's there that I can stop performing and start repenting.

I think it's because He loves me that He makes me aware of my sin; He knows my great need of repentance. I need to be more than an *appearance* of good. The appearances of good are evil when they are only appearances.

Why isn't it obvious that something evil has defined our challenges as physical and not spiritual? As physical bad habits and vices instead of spiritual wickedness? As if lungs, stomach, and liver are more important than the redemption of mind, heart, and soul?

Rewriting God

Trying to make sense of this new spiritual life, I am discovering that my religion can be the busiest part. But those moments I've spent before God, quiet and still, are what I miss most during the busyness.

In a piece of music, the notation for "rest" is a pause in the music. The rest is as important as the note. As John Ruskin explained, "There is no music in a rest, that I know of, but there is the making of music in it."[1] The space that is not filled with music is a space that helps frame the music. It keeps its meter and holds the melody in place. The musical rest is a positive filling of that space, not a void. Just as a decimal point gives structure to math, a rest gives structure to music.

Similarly, the place of solitude is the space where God frames our relationship with Him and directs us in how to play His song. The quiet time I spend with God is a creative space, as positive and with as much substance as any sacrifice of my time, my energy, or my resources.

The composer of the music carefully placed those rests as parts of the whole. To remove them changes everything about the music: its meter, its interpretation, even the melody.

God wrote a piece of music—a symphony, so to speak. Its

notes and directives are contained in His Word. One of those directives is to rest. Christian activity has been editing out these rests, even though God, the Composer, has clearly made a point of their importance, from the commanded Sabbath rest to the solitude Christ modeled for us in such moments as the one depicted in Mark 1:35: "In the morning long before sunrise, Jesus went to a place where he could be alone and pray" (NIV).

Modern Christian culture is changing the song to be more efficient, rewriting God's music and, consequently, changing its melody. Too often it sounds out of sync and out of tune and is hardly recognizable to the original score.

Our confusion is enhanced because, as we rewrite His music, we think we're improving it.

We are called to play His song in our lives as He wrote it and as He intended it to sound. The Holy Spirit conducts this music and helps direct me, keeping me in time with the original score. The pauses for prayer and solitude are not suggestions but requirements. They are not empty spaces to be filled; they are opportunities to hear from God and be refreshed in His presence.

It's here, in this silence and solitude, that we hear the melodies of God, learn His rhythms, and come to know His song.

Blessed Are the Simple

One of the greatest unexpected gifts of having been an artist, writer, and actor is that no one expects people who openly create to be very mature, sophisticated, or even intelligent. Because of this gift, I have experienced more opportunity to exercise child-like freedom without excuse or apology. Part of being childlike is seeing the wonder that blazes all around us. Spontaneously, as they discover His creation, children worship God with a joy that makes most worship services seem tame and mundane, sleepy.

And now I point out that *we* are His children, you and I. And Jesus warns us that unless we change and "become like little children," we can't see and therefore won't enter His kingdom.

We should consider God's idea of growing up. To grow in love would be maturity. To increase in mercy would be responsible; to enlarge our humility, most wise.

It appears to me that the world's expectation of adulthood is to be serious, to remove playfulness, and to forget how to laugh at ourselves. That's why the result of growing up, for many, is the loss of imagination, the death of dreams, and the murder of mystery. And all this is accompanied by the "adult" demand for a god they must understand—a god who ends up looking a lot like themselves.

Blessed are the simple of God . . . because in the mystery of God *everything* is complex, and *nothing* is complex. When we are children, we trust. Everything is beyond our understanding, and the choice becomes simple—to take off our shoes and play in the holiness that surrounds us—with joy.

People Know If It's Love

I have a friend who seems to hate Christians but seems to like me. I imagine he doesn't like Christians because some have been arrogant, judgmental, or unloving—of course, all in the name of God, whose name is Love. My friend reminds me of Ghandi, who said,

"I like your Christ, I do not like your Christians. Your Christians are so unlike Christ."

My friend likes me because he knows I love him.

Please, don't go telling people about Jesus unless you try to love them as Christ does. Believe me, they'll know. You may want to evangelize the world, but you can't do it without loving people.

In Galatians, Paul set us straight: "For in Christ, neither even my best efforts at rule keeping nor my disregard of religion amounts to much. What really matters is something far more important; what counts is far more interior: my faith, expressing itself through love."[2]

Talking about Jesus is not the same as loving like Jesus. And you don't have to be Ghandi to be able to tell the difference.

Using Faith: Believing to Get What I Want

What if to find gratitude—I first need to know loss?

Fallen in a fallen world, I realize that loss is inevitable. But it's often my losses that bring me to God. Unfortunately, loss does not bring everyone to God. Some, when faced with loss, blame God and angrily cling to whatever is left.

But living thankful to God creates a salve that covers the losses that have wounded me, even the sin that has wounded me. They both, in different ways, brought me to know the love of God.

You can tell the people who have been forgiven much. They love much. And they are thankful for much too.

But for now, the not yet and the "Are we there yet?" still haunt me as I struggle to be secure in an unstable world. My demand that God fulfill my every desire has come to be what I consider faith—the faith to believe that God will give me whatever I want. I may pray to God, but I'm only grateful when I get what I want.

Which leads me to a sobering conclusion: it will take greater losses than I have already suffered to gain true gratitude.

But, being grateful, my gratitude has the power to change my attitude. Beauty may move me, but it is *thought* that really changes me. Unless my mind is changed, not much else will follow. Proverbs 23:7 tells us that as we think, so we are.

Again our perception comes into play, shaping our interpretations. For example, consider the interpretation that life seems like a half-full or half-empty glass, depending on how we perceive it. But good—a thankful attitude toward God—can offer hope for the full as well as gratitude for the half-full.

In contrast, evil offers an attitude of self-pity, taking away hope for the full and poisoning whatever is left.

In his book *How Should We Then Live?* Francis Schaeffer concluded (and I'm paraphrasing) that thought and philosophy have been king in changing our cultures. And that, throughout history, music amplified them, and the arts recorded them. He explained, "People are unique in the inner life of the mind—what they are in their thought world determines how they act. This is true of their value systems and it is true of their creativity. This is true of Michelangelo's chisel, and it is true of a dictator's sword. 'As a man thinketh, so he is,' is really most profound."[3]

As I follow Christ, my attitudes are changing, or they should be. Is the change a greater gratitude toward God? Or just a more positive way of viewing the glasses set before me?

The Role We Play

When we walked into the waiting room of the local medical clinic, it was already cast with characters. I could imagine a Broadway play was about to begin. A good play. A play with drama, humor, and absurdity.

While we waited for my grandson Devon's bee sting to be treated, one actor in the waiting-room cast caught my eye. I couldn't tell his ailment, but he appeared to be an artist. At least he looked the part. He wore an artist's tam over his artist-length hair. In one hand he held a blank canvas and with the other, a satchel I was sure held paints and brushes.

Everything about him said *art*. But his canvas was blank.

It made me think of church—or the appearance we take on to "church it up" in our culture, perhaps carrying a big Bible and a satchel filled with tracts and handouts, wearing a large crucifix.

But what do we create? I may have the appearance of an artist, but do I ever paint? I may look like a Christian, but do I ever love?

Honest Doubt Is Still Faith

What if to find faith—I first need to know risk?

Faith requires risk, and only tested faith is a personal possession. As Oswald Chambers put it, "The test will either prove your faith . . . or . . . kill it."[4]

This test of faith proves whether my faith is placed in God or in what I want. The faith that survives this testing is deeply held faith that persists through doubt and still trusts God even when the outcome is not what we hope for.

Don't mistake action for faith. Sometimes action is just the appearance of faith—or even a lack of faith, or a lack of patience, or both.

On the other hand, sometimes *doubt*, of all things, can be a step toward faith. It may seem confusing, but having honest doubt is *not* a lack of faith. I am a man of faith. Some days I face giants and walk into furnaces. Other days I have trouble uttering a simple prayer. I'm still a man of faith—with honest doubt.

Honest doubt *is* faith; lying about faith is real doubt.

Hope for What

Looking back, I can see that what I've called faith has mostly been a hope for my desires. I may have played my faith safe to this point, but now I see that where I risked nothing, nothing was gained. God said that faith is required, not optional, and He isn't pleased without faith.

In how many areas of my life do I live without faith? However many is too many.

I love the writings of Oswald Chambers, even when he gets in my face, as he does here: "Trust completely in God, and when he brings you to a new opportunity of adventure, offering it to you, see that you take it. We act like pagans in a crisis—only one out of an entire crowd is daring enough to invest his faith in the character of God."[5]

Our common sin is self-sufficiency. The common cure for it is faith.

I misuse faith when I use it for the possible or probable, trusting in what I can do instead of trusting what only He can do.

Monet said, "I should like to paint the way a bird sings." It made me wonder what it would be like if my faith created freely, like a bird sings. Trusting, enjoying, and creating with God.

I'm sure it would be impressionistic.

Simple Faith for the Simpleminded

This "loving God for my sake" stage has left me discouraged. My self-directed hope and religion have led me to believe that redemption is in *my* hands and is *my* responsibility, but my experience tells me otherwise. And after my failures as redeemer, I am now discovering a true hope: the hope that the ideas of redeeming myself have all been lies.

Brennan Manning described this absurdity: "Our approach to the Christian life is as absurd as the enthusiastic young man who had just received his plumber's license and was taken to see Niagara Falls. He studied it for a minute and then said, 'I think I can fix this.'"[6]

Until I accept that "I can't fix this,"
that redemption is a process,
that there's sin in this life, and that I am
engaged in a spiritual conflict with that sin,
until then, I live a fantasy.

Now, after failing to fix myself and be holy, I've decided to trust God and stop trying to earn His love. As a result, I think

I'm doing much better with sin. As I continue to taste faith and mercy—whole meals of it—I'm letting God be the author and finisher of my faith.

The test of my faith is whether I come to a quick repentance more than looking for another dose of knowledge. I'm doing my best to keep it simple, following Christ's commandment to love God with my whole heart and to love others as myself. I don't need anything more complex or more difficult to do.

We deny God pleasure by not receiving the joy He offers us.

God wants to enter my reality and make me real. He wants to continue my redemption, as I allow it, and, in the confusion of living, He wants me to trust Him for it.

God also wants me to stop trying to fix everyone else first.

Okay.

False Empathy

Are you my neighbor?

Definitely—especially when I can see you.

If only I can be distracted by some horror taking place in the world I can feel bad about it—and then feel good about feeling bad without ever actually doing anything about it.

I've come to call that response *false empathy*.

I wallow in my emotions while real events take place in my real life, with real people and real situations I could impact for good. But if I only feel awful about a bus crash in Omaha, or only weep about a famine in Africa, and I don't consider the real needs of others in my community, it's false empathy.

This is where I have struggled often in my romantic faith. It's good to *feel* empathy, but true empathy *does* something. Empathy without action is sentimental, lifeless.

Shared need creates community. Where there is little need, there is little community. We are wealthy paupers in relationships—hands too full of things to really embrace each other.

Jim, a missionary in China, told me this story:

It was evening, and he was headed home when, from across the canal, he heard laughter and looked to see several young Chinese men clinging to each other on one bicycle. As they made their own way home through the crowded street, their laughter soothed the long day's work. He knew they were probably headed to a small, shared, one-room apartment in the poorest section of the city. There, covering the floor with their bodies at night, they had found community created through need.

He pointed out that in America we don't share bicycles; most of us have our own cars, and most often we commute alone, rarely sharing a ride with others. Few of us need to share apartments; many of us have our own homes, separate and fenced.

Many believe wealth is always a blessing from God. But the way it sometimes destroys lives, you'd think it was a curse.

Unfortunately, independence also creates no dependence.

Faith in Flight

There is a saying: small target, small miss. It's good advice for aiming but doesn't address what we're aiming at. The problem for us, with God, is that He's constantly on the move. It's my fallen nature that demands a fixed target, one that I don't have to rely on God for, and don't have to trust the Holy Spirit for directions.

My religion often offers to "fix" my targets, and the part of me that is not of God is thankful. One writer explained the problem: "We imagine a target, but it's not the target God is aiming at. So as He lets us fly we cannot imagine we're heading the right direction."[7] As that arrow in flight, I become alarmed because I either see where I'm going and don't like the target, or I can't see where He's sending me. Neither option comforts me like the full knowledge I would prefer or the target I would choose. As God's arrows, we need faith in flight.

A life of faith is like the flight of an airplane: with the earth rotating, the plane is not flying directly at its target; it is flying where its target will be. Likewise, a sailboat is rarely on a true course as it tacks back and forth, using the wind to make its way home. I need more trust and less doubt when He lets me fly and I can't see where He's aiming me.

In this life with God, balance is movement. We are rarely in balance but usually seeking balance. Spiritual balance is found when I stop—or move when Christ moves. I follow the target.

We all struggle with our desire for balance, that place of imaginary security. We all admire balance; we even envy it when we perceive others are living a more balanced life than we. But this balance we see and the balance we desire, is it from God? Is it from a need for God? Or is it personal, prideful gymnastics?

Sin has crippled me. It's as if I am left with one leg to stand on spiritually. My pride, desiring to appear balanced, balances on my remaining leg of abilities, my understandings, even my virtues. It takes all my effort and focus just to maintain this appearance of balance. How long I can continue the effort will depend on my resolve.

Eventually, in exhaustion, God offers me merciful futility. I fall down. Gratefully defeated.

There is an unbalanced balance that pleases God. You see it throughout the Bible. It's only when I accept my imbalance and acknowledge how weak and crippled I am, that I become dependent on God.

That's where I find the paradox of balance, leaning totally on Him.

Snow Flight, 12" x 24"

REFUSING MYSTERY AND CREATING FANTASY FAITH

Everyone wants to understand art. Why not
try to understand the songs of a bird?

—*Picasso*

In art, the background of a painting, as it goes distant, becomes more and more an impression of values, losing many of its details and much of its information. If I create too much information or detail in the background, the painting will appear untrue.

In faith, sometimes my best understandings are only views of distant backgrounds. In this spiritual background I may lose the details, but I should still recognize the values, even though my vision is hindered by mystery. When I create too much information from this background, it isn't faith I demonstrate but the lack of it.

The creation of art is not logical or illogical; it's beyond logic. For artists, problems come when we try to create for our hearts using our head. Some things don't survive the trip.

Similarly, faith is not logical or illogical; it too is beyond logic. For example, there are many songs of mystery, but even if I don't understand the lyrics, I can enjoy the melody. I often create problems for myself when I use my knowledge for faith, because my faith may not survive the trip. Faith is for what is unseen and unknown.

Living by faith can be challenging because my pride is threatened by my faith. My pride insists I know everything, or at least pretend to, all in an effort to maintain the appearance of control.

My pride mocks my faith by creating understandings and refusing mystery.

Imagining My Motives Are Pure . . . Is Imagination

When I take a walk, it's more to think than to exercise. I enjoy that. When Cath walks, it's more to exercise than to think. She enjoys that. To see us walking together you would see a partnership with times of shared silence. On appearance, walking the same direction, with apparently the same purpose, you wouldn't know our goals were different.

In church, we sit in shared rows and face the same direction, apparently in agreement. But what do we *really* share? Or believe? Is it faith, hope, and love?

Are our goals social, clubbish, and nationalistic? Or are our goals God, Christ, and the Holy Spirit?

Maybe my goal is to just look good and feel better about myself. Others wouldn't know as I sit in my row.

It's great fun to question the motives of others, but what motives do I question about myself? That may not be fun at all.

What wrong motives of mine does God want to reveal? And will that revelation lead to repentance?

It's difficult to understand the motives of others. It's even more difficult to understand my own.

To imagine my motives are pure because I feel comfortable is a comfortable deception. And we're more comfortably deceived when those around us sit in similar loungers, watching the same movies, eating the same snacks.

Seeing Sin—but Not Mine

We play golf like we live life. A full round of golf is eighteen holes. You may play great for seventeen holes and keep all the rules, but then there's that one hole . . . the bad hole. Maybe you take a mulligan, a free shot, or maybe you don't count a couple of strokes. Then you proudly add up your score and turn in the card.

We like to keep score in life too. We keep most of the rules, or the rules we choose to keep, or maybe just the ones we *can* keep. You know, the ones that make us feel good about ourselves.

In golf, the lie on one hole makes the total score a lie for the whole round. God said, "If you break one law, you broke them all." He wasn't trying to trick us, just trying to help us see the truth: we need a Savior.

After all, isn't the reason you haven't broken more rules just a mixture of social constraint and cowardice?

Are you convinced you keep the important rules? Or that others' sins are worse than yours? If so, you're not convinced of your own.

God Is Love

"Love covers a multitude of sins."[1]

I first heard Anthony Chapman preach in 1989 while on vacation in York, England. Twice during that sermon I thought, *Woe is me*, and I meant it. He recently taught this: the word *covers* reveals God's heart with a two-part meaning: one, to hide by covering up, and the other, to take or steal. With the understanding that God is love, you could read 1 Peter 4:8 as, "The love of God takes my sin and hides it."

In the story of the prodigal son, that is exactly what the father did when the younger son returned. Weeping with joy, he ran out to him, taking his sin in order to hide it. He covered his son's sin with a robe and his feet with shoes, both hiding the shame of where he had been and what he had done. He then gave him the ring of sonship, restoring his authority as a son.

The father's forgiveness mercifully covered and took away the son's sin. And the father didn't share the young man's sin with everyone but instead asked everyone to celebrate his return. It was time to party!

This stage of loving God for my sake has been an education about God and about my selfishness. As I receive God's forgiveness, He is breaking down the door of my heart with love. Not with a threat or with a battering ram, but with a knock on the door and with the promise that if I open it, He will come in and dine with me.

God has not only forgiven my sin, much of it He hid.

If the prodigal had been frugal
and his morals virtuous,
he might never have returned to his father.

I have great hope for the rebellious prodigal who returns home the fool—
defeated and repentant, grateful for anything
his father might offer.
I fear for the religious older brother who,
thinking himself wise and righteous,
never left home,
never faced defeat,
never had to repent,
And, as a result, is ungracious to his brother
and ungrateful to his father.

There are at least two things that will not polish:
dung and self-righteousness.

What *Should* Surprise Others

Always, Christ told the truth and loved people severely. It's not Christlike to treat people severely and only talk of love.

This journey of "loving God for my sake" has taken me from a prodigal to an elder brother and back again to the prodigal, to . . . am I now again the elder? You get the point. Remember, both

DEEPEST THANKS, DEEPER APOLOGIES

brothers are lost without the love and forgiveness of the Father. Our deceptions as Christians range from imagining we were never a prodigal to forgetting we were.

Jesus described our righteousness, yours and mine, as filthy rags. The rags he describes, however, were used menstrual rags, which sounds disgusting, but disgust wasn't the point. A used menstrual rag held the evidence of unfertilized and stillborn life. The point Jesus was making was that our efforts at righteousness end in death, not life. We cannot create that life; only God can create holiness and righteousness.

Apart from God, all my efforts—even at my very best—will still end in a stillborn death wrapped in rags.

If I didn't know Jesus, I don't think I would want to be a Christian.

We have a huge Christian convention that comes to our area every year. I have Christian friends who work the convention, but it's frustrating for them. Here's why: as a group, these Christians are the most demanding, impatient, and cheap group of all the conventions they work! A lot of their fellow workers don't know God. If God is love, where *is* the love among these "godly" conventioneers? Where's the joy? Where's the kindness? Jesus said, "When you see Me, you see the Father."[2] When people look at us Christians, what do they see?

I'm pretty sure I would have liked Teresa of Avila; she must have been a funny woman and had a great relationship with God, because she would pray, "From silly devotions and sour-faced saints, spare us, O Lord."[3] And given this situation, she might have continued praying, "O saints, please, go and be a blessing to this world and stop being a cheap pain. And smile more." Loving people is our witness. The world should be surprised by our judgment, not by our love.

Wounded by His Love

This stretch of road has been long and tiring. The stage where I love God for my sake has ended with my repentance for trying to use God for His blessings. But I also have received God's love and forgiveness, and because of that, I have discovered I am freer to offer the same to others.

Determined, I have knocked down the old god I created but don't yet realize I'm erecting a new version on the same foundation—my pride. Unfortunately, this idol won't be taken down until later. I am slow, but I am beginning to accept that all my best efforts to save myself have only interfered with God's plan to save me.

God offers me His love even though I have refused to be weak in order to appear strong. Refused His wisdom to appear wise. Refused to be humble to appear confident. Refused to be broken to appear whole. I have even refused to love . . . in order to appear holy.

And yet . . . He forgives me.

I enter a new season with God, wounded by His love.

The Second Prayer

Our Father Who art in heaven, hallowed be Thy name.
Thank You for being my God. I know I can do this—with Your help, of course.

Thy kingdom come, Thy will be done, on earth as it is in heaven.
Would You please help me want what You want? I seem to have a problem wanting Your blessings more than I want You.

Give us this day our daily bread.
I appreciate Your help in all these areas of my life, but I was hoping You could bless me more—You know, just a little more.

Forgive us our trespasses as we forgive those who trespass against us.
I can see how I am wrong sometimes . . . but forgiving everyone? That just doesn't seem right.

And lead me not into temptation, but deliver me from the evil one.
I need Your help, God. I lead myself into temptation and feel that I'm the evil one sometimes. Forgive me for failing. And make me stronger. I promise I'm going to try harder. You'll see.

The Conversion of Brother Lawrence, 20″ x 16″

STAGE THREE

I Love God for God's Sake

Oh, to see, to taste, to feel.

Sensing my mind and spirit are outpaced.

The road blurs with my tears.

And now, on knees knelt,

I'm drawn to remember a place I have only felt.

—*S.C.S.*

Flower Girl, 20" x 16"

THE CONFUSION OF HAVING A
HOLY GOD WHO LOVES ME

*Coming to the end of myself is an illusion that is only broken
by the next time I come to the end of myself. The person in my
mirror, who appears to know himself, is the person who knows he
can't. His only hope is God, the only One who truly knows him.*

—S.C.S.

Now, in stage three, I "love God for God's sake" and think I'm
nearly home. I'm not. Not yet. But I know where I want to go.

The light has become so bright I wish it would blind me so I
wouldn't have to see this. I step out from the shadows and cover
my eyes; I cannot look upon His holiness. But in this honest light,
I clearly see my unholiness.

My hope is turned to fear; my confidence and trust are stripped
away. I am consumed by His glory.

I had no idea what holy was. Lord, have mercy on me!

My selfishness is unknowingly laying waste to all my options except God. My losses have exposed my needs and delivered a strange hope. I feel His presence even in the consequences of my failures.

He still loves me. But for the first time I fear Him because I realize He is Holy, and I am not.

When I came to the end of my bad, I called Him Savior. When I come to the end of my good, I call Him Lord.

Second Repentance

As I begin to love God for God's sake, I have a second repentance—again with tears. But now mind and spirit have been outpaced. I am amazed at how good I am at being bad, and how bad I am at being good.

Watchman Nee told a story about a man who becomes a spiritual man. As we see him sitting in a chair, he looks fine. But once he stands, it's apparent he is clumsy, awkward, and breaks things. While he sat, he *looked* coordinated. It is only when he moves that we see he isn't.[1]

Our new spiritual life with God is much the same. It's uncomfortable, and we make mistakes; we have never been "spiritual" people before. God insists that you and I move, and when we do we are spiritually clumsy and awkward. To be spiritual I must trust and lean on Him for balance, letting Him teach me how to walk spiritually.

Picking Out a New Wardrobe

I now have more hope than doubt, more reality than fantasy, more patience than demands, and more truth about God and myself. I am making peace with paradox, and I receive more of God's love than ever before. That's all good!

And yet . . .

After all this good learning, my first response still remains prideful. I imagine I only need to freshen up my wardrobe, thinking a change of clothes could correct what's wrong with me. Again, it's about my appearance and not about God. By starting the process backward—from the outside in instead of from the inside out—I don't realize it's my unbroken pride that's resolved to do better and try harder.

If I were asked, of course, I would say I believe God did it all. But despite my words, I would admit that, being a responsible Christian, I must do my part. Meanwhile a burning question smolders in my insecure self-esteem: "God, how could I feel good about myself if You *completely* save me?"

I Don't Want Sin—but I Don't Always Want God

One of the greatest fallacies of faith is that I can learn it without living it.

Too often, we prefer to face this life of faith as if it were a geography test about our knowledge of mountains and valleys. But to follow God will mean I climb mountains and descend into valleys. This climbing is harder than imagined, and I *do* descend into valleys more than I first would have believed.

In his book *Beloved*, Henri Nouwen shared about a time when he was personally struggling and was given the rare opportunity of a twenty-minute audience with Mother Teresa. In her presence, he went on for about fifteen minutes pouring out his heart and troubles, and then he stopped and wanted to hear what profound wisdom she would share.

She paused and then said, "If you will spend one hour a day in adoration of your Lord, and you never do anything you know is wrong, you'll be fine."[2]

I can imagine Nouwen saying, "That's it? Really? That's all you got?" Actually, I imagine that's what I would have said.

We all want the secret about a life of faith. Maybe that was it.

> *What God considers paradox, I call contradiction. I see God use paradox to display His splendor; and I seem to use contradiction to display my sin.*

To set a course requires that I know where I am and where I am headed. If my course is for God, it is through His conviction that I have been given the gift of *place*, the "where" I am, and repentance, the heavenly *direction* from my "here." Sometimes this course seems easy, and I want to follow it. Other times I don't. But knowing the way and following the Way are completely different issues.

The consequence of writing about God is that I have come to know myself better: encouraged when I see God in my life and discouraged when I don't. And I have become a scholar, not about *sin*, but about *my* sin. Where the revelations of God have revealed me blind, naked, and a fool, those revelations have also revealed me loved, forgiven, and adopted. The evidence of God in my life is that I don't want sin. The evidence of sin in my life is that I don't always want God.

> *What if to find joy—I first need to know sorrow?*
> *What if to find brokenness—I first need to know betrayal?*
> *What if to know sacrifice—I first need to know selfishness?*
> *What if to find peace—I first need to know fear?*
> *What if to find repentance—I first need to know sin?*
> *What if to find forgiveness—I first need to forgive?*
> *What if to find love—I first need to know God?*

Joy, Sorrow, and the Space Between

What if to find joy—I first need to know sorrow?

We do our best to call happiness joy, and then we get angry that happiness is so fleeting. Joy is not happiness.

Sorrow reveals the shallowness of happiness and proves our need for true joy. It also exposes our search for happiness as desperation and our desire to avoid pain as denial.

Up until now I couldn't have imagined that joy and sorrow might be friends and not enemies. In God's economy, joy and sorrow might be two sides of the same coin—not unlike faith and works. In some ways, the depths of sorrow measure the heights of joy. If I embrace the tragedy of this life, ironically, I also experience greater joy. The greater I experience tragedy and joy, the larger and greater the space that is created between. Not a vacuum but a positive space God will fill with His love.

When the pendulum on a clock swings, it moves fully from one side to the other. Some people live frightened, fearing sorrow and afraid of joy. It's a small safe place they have created, where you are not harmed and do not feel much of anything. It's as if their pendulum has stopped and there is no breadth or span to fill. God lets me embrace joy *and* sorrow with confidence. God creates His love in those spaces of my life, making it a bigger life that can overcome any sorrows and makes joy a second nature.

Here's another contradiction: joy isn't found in attaining; it exists in giving—the exact opposite of all our strategies to become happy. Joy, along with other spiritual gifts, is not so much a gift that's given *to* us as it is a gift given *through* us.

When I think of joy, I think of my grandkids. They exude joy in the simplest ways, unconsciously. God's gift of joy is ready and available to us all the time, but it only exists when I am thankful, not anxious. When I'm a child, not an adult.

I have become more emotional now that I love God for His sake, but I am deceived when I think my greater emotions are greater actions.

Love or Lust?

When art historian Elbert Hubbard said, "There is a difference between loving the muse and lusting after her,"[3] he was speaking to artists about the problems of passion without commitment, and the need of both. He could have also been talking about faith.

I wonder what parts of my faith have been this lusting for God and not a love for God? A romantic feeling instead of obedience. Sentimental intention without sacrifice.

And when I've felt so passionate, why haven't I done more? When I have obeyed, why wasn't it with the greatest of passion? I need both obedience and passion. When I only lust, I am passionate but lazy.

Too much of my faith has been spent living in emotions. I guess I am fairly emotional, for male standards, and being an artist, I find it's easier to hide there as well. Emotions are wonderful and being emotional can give us a sense of being alive. But if I only live in my emotions, I'm not *very* alive.

Sentiments as Real as Sacrifice

If we love as God loves, we will become passionately creative, and our actions will match our words. Our sentiment will be as real as our sacrifice.

This story made me smile: a young woman in a troubled marriage, knowing her parents' marriage wasn't perfect but was full of love, asked her father, "What is the secret of a good marriage?"

"A short memory," he said.

The greater challenge in marriage isn't love but forgiveness. The feeling most newlyweds have for each other is a weak, romantic version of love, well suited for the honeymoon but ill suited for the long haul. It's God's love in and through us that can create *marital love*, which is sacrificial rather than sentimental.

I recently officiated at our friends' twenty-fifth wedding anniversary, where they renewed their vows and confessed to all that without God in their lives their marriage would not have survived. We all watched the fifteen-minute slideshow of their life together as lovers, spouses, parents, and grandparents—beautiful memories, all filled with love. These were life's lovely pictures, but as it would be for all of us, there were other pictures they chose not to show.

First Corinthians 13 says that, when life is all said and done, faith, hope, and love will be all that remains. I imagine heaven has the quality of that anniversary slideshow, showing only the best slides, only the love-filled pictures we have lived. All the rest will be burned away.

Betrayal Must Be Intimate

What if to find brokenness—I first need to know betrayal?

To work as a godly paradox, betrayal must be intimate. Only a deeply loved friend or relative can truly betray us. Friendship shows the depths of beauty; betrayal, the depths of sin. Only a close friend could know the depths of another's beauty *and* his or her depravity.

Christ knows me this well . . . and still calls me friend. He models His command to "love your enemies," by loving *me*.

Betrayal is intimate and personal because it is committed by those we most trust and who most trust us. When betrayal occurs, the temptation in our pride is not to receive forgiveness—or, in our pain, not to offer it. Often when we're betrayed, the pain is so great it reveals our inability to forgive. In a similar way, when we betray others, their pain may be so great no forgiveness is offered—again, revealing our inability to be forgiven without the love of God in our lives.

Being hurt by others can harden a heart, not break it. But when I betray God, my heart breaks, not because of His judgment but because of His undeserved love.

And our hearts *should* be broken—by our own betrayals of others or by their betrayals of us—because only when our hearts are broken can they let God in.

Snowy Day at the Met, NYC, 36" x 36"

WHAT IS WRONG WITH THE WORLD? WE ARE.

I was minding my own business, sitting in church one
Sunday, when temptation took a seat. I was irritated
because it was ruining my mood for worship. Agitated, I
finally demanded to know, "Lord, what is temptation?"

And He answered, "Temptation promises comfort for your self-pity."

—S.C.S.

My self-pity is an enemy to God, a front for my distrust of Him. Self-pity opens the door for temptation, making me receptive to sin.

Temptation will always show up in my life, no matter what, but when I am discouraged and throwing a pity party, temptation is especially powerful. It acts like a comforting friend who understands.

When evil is dressed up as evil, I see it a mile away. But if *I* dress up in evil, get all made up in pity and cloak myself with self-righteousness, I'm blinded. When I look in the mirror I see no evil, even though it may be inches from my face.

Often we have no need of a deceiver; we do quite well on our own.

Standing in front of that mirror, none of us believe we are deceived; how could we? That's the nature of deception.

This maturing in my life of faith has included a new pair of glasses. I used to wear bifocals that made my sin look small and the godly parts larger than they were. I now have better vision with God's new glasses, but I don't always like what I see.

The view reminds me of G. K. Chesterton's answer when he reportedly responded to the question, "What is wrong with the world today?" in a newspaper editorial.

"I am," Chesterton said.[1]

I would agree. *I* am the problem. And you are too.

It's Natural to Be Selfish

What if to know sacrifice—I first need to know selfishness?

I was selfish long before I was sacrificial. The Bible says, "It is better to obey than to sacrifice"[2] because the selfish part of me that doesn't want to obey will go to sacrificial means in order to avoid doing it. When I do make sacrifices, they can have the hidden motives of impressing others or of making me feel good about myself.

I am now aware that my pride and my selfishness are the best of friends, and they would love to ruin any real sacrifice of mine by making sure that I am duly noticed and properly exalted.

My selfishness is also a flirt, and if I'm not paying attention, it can make sin look attractive—and even godly, if the words are persuasive enough. But if I knowingly enter into sin, I feel too uncomfortable to stay in the same room with God. So I step out. Sometimes it's hard to know what the consequences of sin will be. But we *can* be assured of this: sin's first work is always to separate us from God.

I had hoped that loving God for God's sake would finally remove the struggle with sin from my life. But as I continue walking His road, I sense a process that's weaning me from my self-righteousness and challenging my untrusting demands for security. Where the road turns to water will be the place I will finally admit to God, "I can't do it."

And God will answer, "I know. Let Me help you."

Perfectly Imperfect

As an artist I have always been fascinated with artists. Whether I agreed with them or not, they were interesting in spite of their "flaws."

Similarly, the saints I am attracted to have had interesting lives and were also flawed. I take great hope in the flaws of saints; they were people who came to know they were flawed and looked to

God for help. I only have to look at the disciples arguing about who was greatest to understand I *too* could be a disciple.

Passion is imperfect yet often honest.
Perfectionism lacks both passion and truth.

As God's works of art, we are never really finished but instead are in a process that seems imperfect at best. Many years ago, I wrote a children's story titled *Perfectly, Imperfect, Perfectly*. I think this concept aptly describes His creation—and fits most of my experience as well. Until the Perfect returns, we are, for now, perfectly imperfect.

None of Us Is *Always* Anything

In art classes, I was only shown the masterwork of the masters, but later, when I traveled abroad to obscure museums, I found them full of less-than-masterful works by those same masters. As an artist, it was always a relief to me to know the masters were human. Imperfect. They didn't always paint masterwork; in fact, some of it was really awful. What a relief!

We humans don't always create masterwork either. In fact, some of our living has been really bad. And very sad.

Can you accept that you're not perfect and God is?

In this stage, because of our previous failures we keep redoubling our efforts. It's exhausting. And because our focus is still on ourselves, we don't notice the trap our pride has set for us: the sinful desire for our own perfection.

Art: the Signature of Man

Creating art is what I do, not who I am. Creating is what I do for work. It isn't that I'm not grateful to find work that is my passion; it's just that my life needs to be defined by who I am and not by what I do.

I want to honor God in everything I do, whether it's shoveling snow or painting something beautiful. I love creating, but my creations will not love me back. I have known artists who seem to think they will.

Creating is so godlike, it's easy to idolize the creators and worship their creations. In a fallen world, when someone displays incredible talent, the world idolizes that person and offers him or her worship. The temptation for the new god is to accept it.

Our desire to worship creator-people makes some sense to me because there's so much of God showing. Whether or not someone gives God the glory for his or her abilities, those abilities are still gifts from God. But like all good things that He provides, creating is just as easily perverted and misused as any other. Without God, for example, I would use my creativity to create a more beautiful idol.

Creating creates us, or maybe it just reveals us. Chesterton suggested that "art is the signature of man."[3] If that's true, then the creations of man should provide some evidence. And if we could see into the soul of man, based on the evidence, we'd find the most beautiful and the most ugly displayed side by side, hanging in the same gallery. And, if those creations took on life, we would find them dancing together, sometimes even hear them finishing each other's sentences.

This paradox is not easily understood, but it's easily experienced. All of us have some confused understanding when we look at what we have created in our lives—what was good and what was ugly, sitting side by side, whispering.

Created to Create

Creatively and spiritually, ever since we learned to stay in the lines with our crayons, we've struggled to break out. Children create with the freedom that masters only envy, but sometimes, after a lifetime, masters finally, once again, create like children.

As I age, growing into becoming a child of God, I *remember* wonder and experience awe.

As an artist creating, that creating touches something holy in me. It is a part of my who-I-am, and was intended to be. I was created to create as an image bearer of God. My best understanding of that was written by Frederick Buechner: "Literature, painting, music—the most basic lesson that art teaches is to stop, look, and listen to life on this planet. In a world that for the most part steers clear of the whole idea of holiness, art is one of the few places left where we can speak to each other of holy things."[4] Loving God for God's sake is bringing me a new awareness that everything in life has a sense of holiness to it.

In this painting of your life, are you reflecting His holiness?

Imagining: I Am Just, and God Is Not

I went to the Holy Land with our church for the first time a few years back. At the end of our trip we went to the Holocaust Museum. It was a long, narrow, simple concrete structure, a gauntlet of emotions and remembrance, a shrine to what unrestrained evil is capable of. I've seen lots of documentaries, but nothing prepared me for what I saw there. I was overwhelmed by the humanity of it and wrote this:

> In Jerusalem, after nearly two hours of swallowed tears, I found a dark corner and wept ... then left the Holocaust Museum. After witnessing all the photos and memorabilia of murdering Nazis and murdered, discarded Jews ... I left confused. The murderers didn't look like monsters, and the murdered looked like my neighbors' children. God, how could this be?

When evil has been successfully evil, its next hope is to lead those who survived into believing they are just—and God is not.

I see a lot of us trying to fight evil. Some, in our own strength; others, actually hunting for it. But the best analogy I've ever heard about dealing with evil was given by my South African pastor, Gary Fox. He said (I'm paraphrasing) it's like walking a path through the bush in Africa. The path is narrow, and you carry a large stick because a snake may cross your path and you will need to kill it. You keep your eyes out for snakes that may be hiding as you walk, and you stay on the path. You don't start poking the bushes with your stick, looking for snakes. You don't leave the path and walk in the bush where they live.

God gives me the authority and the power to stand against evil. I need to stay on His path and remain aware that an enemy lurks nearby, hoping to catch me off guard. I must be ready with my "stick."

All the Senseless Beauty

Hawaii is a place of extraordinary beauty and temperate peace. I love being there. It feels heavenly.

But I couldn't live there because I know it's an island. I prefer larger islands, like North America. Nearly every morning when I'm in Hawaii, I get up before sunrise. I think and pray as the sun rises and the surf plays. Sometimes whales perform to seagull songs, and the shells applaud with every wave that moves them.

Sometimes I watch and think, *All this senseless beauty . . . wasted on me.*

Why, God? The rising sun, the singing birds, the offshore breeze that feathers the waves, the surf that plays through the rocks—why all this beauty, when the times it's noticed are only moments? It comes and goes, even when no one sees; His beauty continues, relentless, senseless, extravagant.

In remote mountain meadows—more senseless beauty. There, God's extravagant beauty carpets the earth with wildflowers. All different in kind and color. *Wouldn't simple daisies do, Lord?*

God's beauty is only senseless because I am. His beauty goes unnoticed because I am the fool to not see. Because I'm not still and quiet enough to notice. Not child enough to care.

God, help me. Forgive me. Help me make sense of this senseless beauty.

Me to God, Not God to Me

One morning in Hawaii, in the dark, after I quietly got everything together to leave for the beach, I couldn't find the car key. I looked everywhere it should have been, and then I looked everywhere else. Still no key. I was about to give up and stay home when I felt the key in my pocket.

During all the searching, I had forgotten I already had it. I possessed what I thought was lost; the whole time I searched, carrying with me what I needed most.

Sometimes I forget I already know God, even though I see Him in every sunset—a new self-portrait every day. I touch His hand when I hold my grandchild's.

I know Him. I have received His Spirit, and I know my sins have been forgiven in Christ. I don't need to search any longer. God promised that. He's already given me everything I need. When I don't believe and accept that's true, I act like the confused Christian described by Watchman Nee: as a man trying to break into a room he is already in.[5]

I need more solitude with God, not less.
The purpose of solitude is not for a vacation
but for a preparation.
And what it prepares us for is a sacrifice.

I wish my theology matched my faith. Often it doesn't. It's a process of alignment. Part of that process is the testing of my faith.

I try to understand life without God or His Word. I try to make sense of things using the logic of men. But after all the testing, I come to find that man's logic tastes bland, unsatisfying, same.

When I was young and had a metabolism, I used to surf in Baja. I remember going into a bakery one day and finding dozens of great-looking pastries, all different in color, size, and shape. I bought several of the best-looking ones and greedily left. But when I started to eat them, I was shocked to discover that they all tasted the same—and not good. Or even sweet. The bakery seemed to have created the pastries without sugar or chocolate, and hid that fact with color and design. The baked goods had lots of color but no flavor. The "chocolate" was only brown.

Now, when I see an enticing display of man's philosophies, I am reminded of that pastry shop in Baja, recalling how beautiful the pastries appeared but how bland they tasted.

In the same way, man's colorful philosophies are seductive, but they are not good, and not sweet.

The good news is that we were created to enjoy what is good, what is sweet, and what satisfies. But it is only God who makes good on His promises. Only God can be trusted to ensure that what we see and what we get are one and the same.

Hidden Reefs of Pain

On a family retreat in Hawaii, I was bodysurfing with my grandson Cade when he asked, "What makes waves?"

I grew up surfing in Southern California, so I'm familiar with waves and their structure. But for my grandson I simplified my answer to, "What happens on the surface is caused by what's on the bottom. A swell may cross the entire ocean before it breaks on this shore. The larger waves break farther out on hidden reefs."

Here's the metaphor:

We all see the struggles on the surface, but we don't see the causes that lie beneath.

Sometimes as we swim through life there's apparent peace. The waves are small, the sun is shining, and the beach seems predictable. We enjoy feeling that we're in control.

But other times there's a storm at sea, and far away the ocean begins to throw off swells that aren't noticed until they reach *our* beach. Only when they reach land do we discover their true size. Until they do, we can't imagine a problem because the sun may still be shining, the birds may be singing, and we may feel like we're in control. But out there beyond the horizon, the swells are growing in size. Before we know what has happened, they may become massive and unexpectedly crash on hidden reefs of hurt and disappointment we didn't even know existed.

Some people are lost or drowning in that kind of stormy surf.

I can't see the bottom of other people's lives. I can't even see the bottom of my own. But what I can do is offer grace and compassion to others—and, I hope, with God's help, even to myself.

I am beginning to understand that God's command to "love your neighbor as yourself" includes loving myself as a neighbor.

Offshore Wind, 12″ x 16″

LOVING MYSELF AS
MY NEIGHBOR

We have all forgotten what we really are. All that we
call Spirit and Art and Ecstasy only means that for one
awful instant . . . we remember that we forgot.

—G. K. Chesterton, Orthodoxy

The year 1982 was an interesting one for me. I was closer to God than I had ever been before, learning more than ever about this life of faith. But everything I was learning was challenging what had been before. And then, I faced the challenge of being an actor in Hollywood. Some people don't think Christians belong there, but I, for one, am grateful that Pat Boone was there.

Please allow me to take a little diversion here to share a brief history of my spiritual life. I grew up in the Methodist church—confirmed at twelve, agnostic at seventeen. As a young man, I saw the injustice and lovelessness of the many religions, and I blamed God for them all.

In 1975, with the encouragement of Cath and friends, I went to Calvary Chapel in Costa Mesa. In time, and by God's mercy, I reconciled my life to God. Shortly after that, Cathy and I were married.

Modeling, acting, and New York followed, and along the way, I strayed from God. Two years later, in 1979, I was back in L.A. as the new "sweathog" replacing John Travolta when he left the TV series *Welcome Back, Kotter.*

Shortly after that, I met Pat Boone at a celebrity event, and he invited me to Church on the Way, where Jack Hayford was the pastor. It was there that I began to understand what a godly man was supposed to look like. It was there that I was given the hope that God would never be disillusioned with me—because He was never under any illusion in the first place. (Thanks, Pastor Jack.)

In the years since then, I have had great teachers and friends. Despite what I learned along the way, as I grow older, my revelation is not how strong I am becoming, but how weak I have always been.

In those early years, the spiritual life was a different life, and I didn't understand much. In 1981 I was co-starring with Debbie Reynolds in another TV series called *Aloha Paradise* when Dean Jones came in to guest-star. It would be the first time I ever took God to work with me.

We filmed at Universal Studios, and the first day on set Dean came to my dressing room, and we prayed. Just like in church. I didn't know you could do that! Then, together, we walked the sound-stage perimeter, praying for God's presence and protection.

I have to admit, it seemed strange, and I was glad no one really noticed what we were doing.

Before that day, I imagined, as I reached the guard gate to the Universal lot, that God was required to get out of my car. And out of my life. The realization that God could be involved with every part of my life was something that had never occurred to me. (Thanks, Dean.)

I have lots of stories of those years. Some are good; some are bad. All are redeemed.

Why would I envy other people?
They might only be hiding their fears and
failures better than I do.

In 1982 I stood at a crossroads with Captain Purdell, an English fool for Christ, in his full Salvation Army uniform. There we were, armed only with a small amplifier, the gospel, and smiles. The range of responses to our message was telling. Some people changed course to keep their distance. Some passed by gratefully; others, angrily. Still others passed obliviously. And then there was the occasional toss of a penny from a passing car.

As I stood at that intersection, I was aware that my acting agents were in the high-rise building across the street, my accountant was in the building just above me, and countless people were going their own ways around me. But going where? I wondered. Did I care? Did I believe they were on their way to an eternity separated from God?

On that corner, at the same time, I stood at another crossroad—a spiritual one—where God revealed the lovelessness of my heart.

I was on the Salvation Army board at the time and was always amazed at the patience and concern that Captain Purdell had for the damaged, homeless, and downtrodden, especially when so many of them were often demanding and rude. I didn't understand, until one evening when he prayed before we left to feed the homeless, "Lord, we bring You soup . . . we bring You sandwiches."

God's Peace or Mine?

What if to find peace—I first need to know fear?

The Bible says we are not to be anxious, but aren't we? Jesus called anxiousness sin. We call it being responsible. And if not responsible, a reasonable fear.

Personally, I have a problem with peace. I want peace like others might want a new car. Because of that, I am in danger of longing for peace instead of longing for God. I face the temptation of indulging myself with peace that *I* can provide.

In this life, it's easy to find fear. It's not easy to find peace—unless you make an idol of it.

I have lots of strategies to find my peace and avoid my fears, all without the need for God. But if I've found peace, and I want God, I need to ask its source. *Is it me, God, or something else?*

Does my quest for peace cause me to deny God to avoid conflict? Is that the cost? Is it peace that requires some conditions or circumstance, where I am only peaceful when my expectations are met? Or maybe it's a peace that comes at the expense of reality, where I deny my fears by pretending in life.

God's peace that passes my understanding is peace that trusts Him in any situation in spite of conflict. In spite of outcome.

If I lack struggle, it's not necessarily evidence of peace . . . but perhaps evidence of death.

"Honestly" Is Excellence

If God showed us perfection, it was when Jesus offered a child as the model for what it takes to enter the kingdom of God: the faith of a child, the humility of a child, and the simplicity of a child. Not perfection, not excellence, not sophistication.

Instead of worrying about what you don't have, take what you do have and give it your best effort. Henry Van Dyke encouraged us: "Use what talents you possess: the woods would be very silent if no birds sang there except those that sang best."[1] God would not refuse our offerings any more than we would refuse a song performed by our children.

We often misuse the concept of excellence, especially in worship. Instead of offering ourselves to our Savior, we offer ourselves to a standard. We should approach God as a child and not as a professional when we sing our song of worship. Imagine potential as a piece of marble. When Michelangelo finished "David," it was still the same marble, but it was now a masterpiece. What potentials are you hiding?

When it comes to our abilities, there's really no way to know what emerging talents today could develop into mastering beauty tomorrow. It took ten years before I learned how to paint as I wished. And as a writer, I am better today than I was last Tuesday.

Everyone is given potentials, but few work hard enough to develop them. The question I would ask is this: God has given you gifts; why don't you offer them to Him . . . as you are . . . as your gifts exist today?

Offer them simply, humbly, and in faith, even when they aren't what the world considers excellent. When we give God our honest worship, it should be as simple as a child's. Your Daddy Father will enjoy *any* dance, *any* song, and *any* thoughts you'd like to offer Him. Honestly *is* excellent.

Consequence and disobedience know no "stages." Reaping what I sow spiritually goes way beyond my present consequence. God created Creation . . . and creating continues Creation. Life in all its forms experiences a continuing birthing process.

Any time, any day, I am capable of experiencing all the stages because the stages are only reflecting my choices and their consequences.

My Religion an Idol?

At some point, maybe now, I am having a crisis in my faith. I'm at a place where my soul longs to offer more than my religion requires. And where I wonder if the good that is acceptable to others may not be the good of God. I have a growing fear that my religion could be an idol. It's a good crisis, creating a question that needs to be answered.

My hope was that the spiritual life would be more like higher education, something I could measure. In reality, it's been more like the weather, both challenging and surprising. For those closest to me, I'm sure I've been weather, and not always fair.

Our lives are parables to others. They watch to see not just the story of our lives but the truth of it. In the parable of *me*, what will others read today? What was read yesterday?

It isn't that practice makes perfect but that my practice makes *permanent*. With God, my *practice* in this life will always be imperfect, but what I practice will *become* permanent, whether it's love for God and man or efforts to attain the perfection of being proud and permanently selfish.

People only read our actions and only hear what we do.

Who Am I?

If you were to visit my studio, you would first notice the clutter—pictures and sketches lying on the floor. They are there because I'm afraid I'll forget them. You would also notice pictures of family, friends, and memories all over the walls and furniture. If I put them away, I'm afraid I will forget them too, or at least some of them. And I don't want to forget *any* of them. They help me remember not only who *they* are but also who *I* am. And I need to remember that.

I need to remember who I am when I am tempted.

I need to remember who I am, and not forget.

Forgetting is bad, but forgetting you forgot . . . tragic.

The things in my studio help me to remember. The smiling pictures of my kids, grandkids, parents, and friends. Pictures of Cath as a four-year-old—and on our wedding day. The tapestry above the door, "The Lord Will Provide," and a host of saints on bookshelves all keep watch over me, helping me to not forget.

I need to be reminded I belong to Christ and that I am a husband and a father, a son, a brother, and a friend. I must remember—who I am, who God is, and who I am to be.

This is my cloud of witnesses.

Weakness as Strength

The lesson of a long life is to finally understand it is your strengths and not your weaknesses that betray you. George MacDonald reminded us that "every man is open to commit the fault of which he is least capable."[2] Most people doubt they could be capable of such faults. I have no doubt about how capable I am.

In youth, I only thought about my strength, only wanting to be stronger.

Now older and maybe wiser, I see my weakness and realize my strength is hopeless. In truth, I now only have enough strength to embrace God, His strength sustaining me. His embrace, the surer hold.

We build defenses for our weaknesses, not for our strengths. That is why we are weakest where we think strongest.

I am hopeless without God. He said, "My grace is sufficient for you, for my power is made perfect in weakness."[3] I find it hard to convince people I am weak. They imagine I am merely being humble. I am not. To become weaker as God gets stronger is a paradox. But it is a paradox that encourages me.

More and more, I don't strive as much at pretending to be strong. I'm constantly and pleasantly surprised that God isn't surprised at my weakness. In fact, He encourages it, wanting me to be fully aware of just how weak I am so I might cling to Him more tightly. Desperately.

Deciding to write about God was a sobering consideration for me because I know how weak I am. But if it's true that He is strong in my weakness, then I approach each page from a place of strength—His. And with "fear and trembling" I will work out my salvation by writing—trembling because I *do* fear God in the best of ways.

Shrines or Altars?

My past is filled with sins I called mistakes. It took a long time for me to admit my sin was not simply a mistake, that it was me, alone, sinning against a holy God, and not some part of a larger conspiracy. Over time, I "perfected" those mistakes. As comedian Peter Cook said, "Oh, yes. I've learned from my mistakes . . . and I'm sure I could repeat them exactly."[4]

As funny as that remark is, our sin is not funny; it carries devastating consequences. Until I admitted my mistakes were sin, I needed no forgiveness—and didn't receive any. When I offered God my sin, not my mistakes, He forgave me.

My past is memory now, but my enemy wants to rewrite my history. Will I let him? It's true: I am a sinner saved by grace, but there's a deeper truth . . . that I am God's beloved. Who will I choose to believe, God or the devil?

Whose story am I now a part of? God has written a new story for me that has a new beginning and end. A story for today and forever. It's my story—a true story and not fiction—my story of redemption.

I must decide what to remember of my memories. Do I remember God's forgiveness and mercy more—or my failure and sin? Both are true, but one is truer.

The past facts in our lives stay the same, but we shouldn't. We should break all relationship with guilt and shame, refusing to listen to their accusations. And even though, at this stage, we are freer to live and to love, guilt and shame delight in dropping by for unannounced visits.

God has forgiven my past and promised me a glorious future, but my present battle is not just believing in God but believing He loves me. Just as I am.

Our lives are filled with successes and failures of all kinds, and it's there, especially at the successes, that we tend to build our "monuments." But I agree with William Faulkner that these places should be considered markers rather than monuments[5], the difference being that monuments in our lives imply a false sense of completion while markers are more truthful and healthy. A marker indicates, "This is not just how far I have come but where I stopped and started again."

Very little of this life is finished; most of it is in process. Most everything about God is movement, alive and growing. Most everything about evil is stagnant and dead—or dying. A life of faith is a continuing movement toward God where I create markers reminding me of His love and forgiveness, and not monuments to my sin and rebellion. Monuments should be markers, and sometimes markers are altars.

Freed from My Tyranny as God

The stage of "loving God for God's sake" has been an education by the Spirit of God. And the bulk of that education has exposed my self-righteousness.

After years of faith it seems I should have higher degrees, not just in love and forgiveness, but also in recognizing pride and self-righteousness. Seeing yourself in God's light is a blessing that can feel like a curse.

At this point in the journey, personal failures and my disappointment with others have exposed my outwardly godly life as self-serving behavior with questionable sacrifices. Continuing to move toward God will require more humbling.

On my way to speak to a men's group, the accuser had my ear, discouraging me and calling me hypocrite and worthless. I told my wife, Cath, what was going on, and she said in the most sincere and loving way, "Who better than you to speak of sin, forgiveness, and God's love?" (Thanks, honey.)

The devil hasn't stopped reminding me of my sins, calling me hypocrite and worthless. But the Holy Spirit keeps reminding me that Christ calls me His beloved and that I am forgiven. I like the way God tells my story.

It is at this point in faith that God wants to, as Oswald Chambers might put it, "hurt your sin to death."[6] It takes a lot to get us there, to finally come to the end of *our* faith, *our* religion. At that point we thirst for God and *mostly* nothing else.

During this stage, of loving God for God's sake, I am discouraged to find many of my efforts failing. It's been painful to watch the agonizing death of my self-righteousness; I thought he was one of the nicest people I've been. I am beginning to "misunderstand a little less completely," and now feel myself filling with hope—that my *self* must die to free me from my tyranny as *god*.

A Storehouse of God's Love

God hears my prayers, and He answers, but insists my guilt and shame must leave to make room for His love and forgiveness. Their departure is required because living for Him requires that my life becomes a storehouse of His abundant love, preparing me to freely receive His love so that I can freely share it.

I now weep more, and laugh more. I now feel more able to forgive others—because I see my own frailty in them. And more able to forgive, not because I pity *them*, but because I pity *us*. A deeper understanding of God is a deeper understanding of love.

Grateful, but still unsure how this is going to happen, I dry my face and press on . . . to where the road is turning into water.

The Third Prayer

Our Father who art in heaven, hallowed be Thy name.
You are holy, God. Forgive me for not knowing that. And thank You for Your patience.

Thy kingdom come, Thy will be done, on earth as it is in heaven.
I surrender to Your coming kingdom. And in the meantime, Your will be done on earth as it is in heaven.

Give us this day our daily bread.
Forgive me for squandering so much of what You've blessed me with.

Forgive us our trespasses as we forgive those who trespass against us.
Forgive me for not forgiving. I had no idea how bad things were inside me, until now.

And lead me not into temptation, but deliver me from evil.
I need Your help, God. I can't seem to live this life of faith. Have mercy on me. Please.

Running With the Wind, 40" x 30"

STAGE FOUR

I Love Myself for God's Sake

See the sun meeting the sea—
Where my rainbows end.
That's where my Love waits for me.
And only Love has prevailed,
Only Love has truly seen
Where my road has turned to water,
I have received Your love for me.

—*S.C.S.*

Veritas, 36″ x 48″

10

RECEIVING GOD'S FORGIVENESS AND LOVE: STRENGTH FOR THE JOURNEY

After a lifetime of faith
one of the greatest acts of faith
is to believe that God really loves us,
precisely because we now have enough faith
to believe He really does know us.
God, if You say that loving me pleases You . . .
then please do.

—S.C.S.

There is a road that leads to love—not self-love but God's love.

Lord, You say these wonderful things about me. Are they true?

I have faced and overcome many obstacles, and there will be more, for sure, but now God wants me to see that my last conceit to be dealt with is self-hatred. Like a stowaway, it has hidden itself on this passage and now comes out from hiding, appearing to look humble and acting contrite. But it's nothing more than my disenchanted self-righteousness, trying to look godly.

As I continue moving toward God, I approach the place where this life is growing "strangely dim"[1] in the bright-reflected light sparkling at the end of this road. I'm growing tired of this game; the music has stopped, and I have no chair. After a lifetime, the party is finally ending, and I'm relieved.

As I look back, it all seems like such a masquerade. Fighting a religious hangover, I know that whatever I've had of God, I need something *new*, something *more*. The ache in my soul is for God alone. But even though people may think well of me, God and I know I haven't given my whole heart . . . not yet.

Why not? I wonder. The question haunts me.

Guilt and shame no longer paralyze me, but I sense there's still another lesson I must learn. I ask the Lord, "What do You want of me?" He answers, "To do justice, love kindness, and walk humbly with your God."[2]

And then He asks me a question: "When will you let Me love you? When you think you're good enough or deserving enough? You must let Me love you as you are."

I ask, "But what can I offer in return?"

This time He insists, "You *must* let Me love you as you are."

Where the Road Forks

Being born again is not a religious slogan but a requirement of God. I was born naturally into sin and need to be born again of God, in a supernatural spiritual way.

It's a naïve hope that my natural life only dies a natural death. It's a desperate maturity that accepts that natural life must die a holy death. And only God, as I allow Him, can help me sacrifice my natural life for His spiritual life.

This stage, where I love myself for God's sake, isn't heaven, and I haven't reached where the road turns to water yet either. But after all this time on the road, it feels heavenly. The pressure I used to feel to perform for others or to conform to the group has weakened. I've grown weary of religious games, and my allegiance is shifting to God. I've been surprised to discover that not everyone crying, "Lord, Lord!" knows God. I want to make sure I'm one who does.

Though I could still return to the other stages, the longer I am here, at the stage where I love myself for God's sake, the more I want to stay. I have found freedom here because my pride and selfishness have little strength while my passions are being filled by God. With a patience that is not mine, I find I am in no hurry to leave.

Finally, after all my efforts to give something, I understand I must receive. After spending my life in effort, I am finally accepting the true gift of helplessness—my opportunity *and* my need to receive.

To love myself for God's sake is my surrender to receive everything from God.

It's taken me a lifetime to accept this truth and will require daily reminding. Why did I resist accepting this beautiful love He's always wanted to give me?

Now, with God's help, I have answered God's question, "When will you let Me love you?" with my answer, "Please, now."

Why didn't I start this way? I guess that's part of the mystery, but looking back, I can't imagine it happening any other way.

When I first met God, I wanted to use Him—and was humbled.

When I discovered He was holy, my lying pride tried to serve Him—and I was broken.

So we now have the truth about life, about God, and about ourselves. God is holy. God has been waiting to show His strength in my weakness. So isn't my need for God complete? Isn't this the place we want to be? Isn't this the goal of the journey?

Unfortunately, I think this is where the road forks, and I have the option of taking the business route back through stage two or three. How many self-righteous attempts does it take until my foolishness is completed? Only God knows. But I know now that self—*my* self—is the person who can't tolerate being broken, hates being contrite, and denies depravity. Self wants nothing to do with my loving myself for God's sake. Because if I do that, my selfish *self* will be doomed.

We all need help sometimes from a friend, a therapist, or a book. But in this case, God has to be my healer. This is work that can't be done by a pastor, a counselor, or a writer. Nothing can replace God and His Word.

None of us want to stay broken and contrite, especially when brokenness or contrition is caused by our own failures. But that extreme need, the need for God alone, is exactly what you and I need when we're broken and humbled.

The times in my life when I've been desperate for God have been terrible times. The challenge I see now is to need God that desperately without my life being turned upside down or inside out. Father, how can You make me a saint *without* the upheaval? How could I ever have come to need You without it?

The mood is broken as my self begins the argument that religion wants me to at least *appear* whole. To be broken and humble in church doesn't look very victorious; being contrite lacks the confidence of a good witness, right? Since I am already practiced in appearances, it just makes sense at this point to turn back.

Like a roller-coaster cresting, I once again promise, "I will do my best, Lord, to create *my* holiness for Your glory."

If only we could stay at this stage and trust God as we are, truly believing He loves us as we are.

Merciful Wounds

I'm not sure when I last tried to be strong, tried not to feel so weak. Maybe it was today. Why *this* battle? Why now? Why here, when I've come so far?

But unlike so many other times before when I didn't understand, *this* time I see the paradox of this battle: unless I stay weak, I will not let God be strong. I must choose who will be strong. Me, or God? Who do I want to fight this battle?

What I had considered weaknesses, God has redeemed. What I had wanted to run from, God has brought me through. He is my strength and my shelter. And He is creating His life in me by creating wisdom from the ruins of my failure. He is wounding my pride with love, creating humility.

We all suffer wounds of sin, wounds from others, and wounds that are self-inflicted. But we are unprepared for the wounds of love from God. He wounds us with love so that we will be hindered from sinning, weakened so we can receive His strength. Another paradox.

What the world considers weakness and flaws, God has redeemed and made beautiful. Jacob was blessed with a limp. What are you blessed with? Do you consider it a blessing?

Merciful Futility

Finally, I see the paradox that:
Through my darkest despairs You light my life with hope.
What I thought lost, You had mercifully taken.
The betrayals of others hardened my heart,
but my betrayal of You has broken it.
I was blinded with selfishness,
but You healed my eyes to see.
My sorrow is becoming Yours—as well as my joy.
My sin that I tried so hard to wash and tried so hard to outrun
has finally caught me.
But instead of the judgment I deserve,
You offer me love.
I love You too.

The light seems brighter, and yet the mystery has increased. I squint, and a smile crosses my face. Yes, I'm still in a land of paradox, but I think I can see where the road is turning to water. There have been many trials, but I'm beginning to understand that the greatest trial may not be ahead of me but rather here, walking with me in my shoes.

Accept Forgiveness and Repent

What if to find repentance—I first need to know sin?

When sin gave birth in my life, it brought death. I knew I couldn't save myself; I needed a savior. But when I finally looked to God for help and asked Him to forgive me, I was surprised to find He already had. My repentance didn't cause God's forgiveness.

I came to realize I could only accept His forgiveness, not create it. I couldn't earn His forgiveness—even by repenting.

Sin wasn't missing in my life. Sin has always been part of my life—a family heritage. But to really know sin required some familiarity, even intimacy.

My desire to repent and change is born out of gratitude. I keep wanting to obey because I am thankful. I love God because He first loved me. I wonder if religion has gotten this backward: Maybe it's not repent and be forgiven. It's accept His forgiveness and live repentantly.

Did You Say You Sin?

Episcopalians weekly (or more often) confess their sins to God and to each other publicly. I find that beautiful and healthy, even holy. This is one of the "Confessions of Sin" from the Episcopal *Book of Common Prayer*:

> Most merciful God, we confess that we have sinned
> against you in thought, word, and deed, by what we
> have done, and by what we have left undone. We have
> not loved you with our whole heart; we have not loved

our neighbors as ourselves; we are truly sorry and we humbly repent. For the sake of your Son Jesus Christ, have mercy on us and forgive us; that we may delight in your will, and walk in your ways, to the glory of your Name. Amen.[3]

On occasion my older friend Don and I visit the Episcopal service. It's a great place to pray because it's so peaceful and reverent. As I sit there and take communion, served every time, I feel respect—and some fear—toward a holy God. I know Jesus is closer than a friend,[4] but I'm still not comfortable treating God as my "bowling buddy."

You would label me an evangelical, yet my soul is attracted to this kind of liturgy. It's our hearts that decide what makes a ritual holy or meaningless, real or religion. Evangelicals seem to avoid rituals, but it has always seemed strange to me that you could go your whole life as an evangelical without ever publicly admitting your sin.

Why is that?

When We Are "gods"

Man's religion, the self-righteous version, has always been with us and will be until Christ's return. In this book's introduction I said I still have a dull fear that I'm being seduced by the world and betrayed by my religion. We know the world seduces. What we often don't understand is that religion can seduce us too.

I enjoy freedom of faith, but I always have to consider whether my freedoms are becoming a license to sin. I have attended fellowships and gathered with many different kinds of Christians, all of whom seem to have their own flair for rules. What one group declares off limits, another is all right with, and so on and so on. What's interesting to me is that all are sincere about their different conclusions, and all use the same Bible to support their beliefs. Some won't drink or smoke but then indulge in donuts and are addicted to caffeine.

> *With God, there is a peace that passes performance—and in the face of "man's religion," a love that endures all appearances.*

I'm not attacking any particular vices you may have; I have my own. What I want to make clear is that Jesus said that *nothing* should dominate our lives except our love for Him. And He made it clear that when I overindulge in anything, it is a form of gluttony, whether it is donuts or organic health food.

We spend far too much time deciding on the rules we author rather than obeying the rules Christ authored: to love your enemy and to love your neighbor as yourself.[5]

At one point, I was in fellowship with people who were big on euphemisms. They spent a lot of effort guarding their speech and worrying about the interpretation of words. For example, they imagined "cussing" as using words other than cuss words. They had no idea that when I said "darn," I didn't mean "damn," or that when I said "gosh," I had no thought of God or of taking His name in vain. And they really would have been surprised what I meant when I said "that's nice!"

The real language we speak is from our hearts and is clearly interpreted by God. *He* understands perfectly.

I won't swear and take God's name in vain, but the cuss words still roll through my mind and on occasion surface from my heart through my mouth. Usually not in public, but in private—like when I am writing a book about God on the computer. My computer skills are so advanced, I can lose whole paragraphs and pages when I least expect it. This causes those words to "come forth." But because I am writing about God, I catch them quickly and repent: *C'mon, Steve, what are you doing, talking like that? God, I'm sorry. Forgive me.* Then I consider standing before Him, another Adam in a different garden, saying, "God, it's that computer You gave me."

"It's the problems I face."

"It's the injustice I suffer."

Like Adam, I stand before God not wanting to admit my sin. Like Adam, I'm quick to offer an excuse or blame someone else for my behavior.

Without God's priority to love, even my opinions about Him can create fortresses of doctrine that I must defend. Once it's built, I defend my own fortress of theology instead of actually following God. The longer I stay, the higher the walls grow—as if to keep God Himself in . . . or out. Have you ever noticed that prisons look like forts?

It's no wonder we're so vulnerable to seduction. With the right set of rules—rules that accommodate our personal tastes—we can soar to great heights in the local sanctuary. But with little of God in them, exhausted, we hit the sanctuary floor.

Sooner than later we all crumble under the weight of that world we have created. God mercifully lets our world come apart so that He can put it back together . . . His way.

Failure is one way out of man's religion because failure forces the real issues of faith. When I can't keep the rules, do I run *from* God or run *to* Him? When I leave man's religion, am I open to God's?

The Freedom to Love

Christ said He was about mercy, not religion. He died to free me from condemnation and from the seduction of man's religion, which removes my need for God by making *me* god.

To follow Christ in freedom is a great challenge. He set us free and commanded us to first love God, then to love man.

And all this without ever mentioning a denomination.

As I continue to live this life of faith, I am reassured by His promise that He will finish what He has begun in me, because I can't seem to do it on my own.

To Forgive Is Not Just; It's Divine

What if I first need to forgive—to know forgiveness?

What if the first person who needs God's forgiveness is me? And what happens if I don't accept it? Do I hate myself? If I block God's forgiveness to me, does that block my forgiveness to others?

God's love is limitless, unconditional, and I need it to truly forgive others. God said His forgiveness requires that I forgive others.

If I refuse to forgive others, I refuse His forgiveness to me. In loving myself for God's sake, I realize I have been given so much of His love that it's much easier to pass that love on to others. The more I love and forgive others, the easier it is to love even more.

There are still times I struggle to forgive, times when I feel unable to forgive. But whenever I try to justify my lack of forgiveness, God's Spirit reminds me that forgiveness is not justice. How very glad I am that it's not.

Solitude, a Place for Heaven

I have a cabin that sits on the shore of heaven and earth where, in that quiet (*if* I'm quiet), I can hear bird feathers in flight and unknown rhythms of lapping water. Where, without a sound or warning, the unseen wind licks the lake like a flame and ignites the surface, spreading like a wildfire.

I am broken by your beauty, O God.
I bow down before You in worship. This desire of peace,
is it heaven?
Or just a glimpse of it?
But I also hear an anxious mind, a restless heart, and a groaning soul.
Not unlike the beauty surrounding me, I too long to be redeemed.
Lord, I find You in this solitude and understand why the world
    goes mad . . .
If there's no time for quiet, I don't think—I fear.
If there's no time for peace, I don't worship—I demand.
And if there's no time for solitude, I don't pray—I despair.
To hear God requires a quiet place.

But when I finally find the quiet, I hear You say, To hear Me only
    requires a quiet soul.
In the psalms, You said, "Be still, and know that I am God."
When I am still . . . I know.

The biblical practice of fasting from food is as good for the soul as it is for the body. Solitude is the fasting of time, minutes or hours I purposely set aside for God; it is good for the soul, and studies indicate it is good for the body as well.

I seek solitude every day and find it often beside the lake or in my sauna. Both places have doubled at times as prayer closet and writing studio, where much of this book was written.

In my life I have to set aside time for God because if I don't, my time gets filled to the brim with everything but God. Physically, that kind of busyness is like being buried up to my neck in sand; spiritually, it's like being buried headfirst.

The more solitude in nature,
the farther you can hear.
Maybe that's why, in solitude with God,
we can hear from great distances—
maybe even as far as the closeness of
heaven . . . or the distance of my own heart.

Surprisingly, Charles Wagner said in 1901, "The man of modern times struggles through a maze of endless complication."[6] For me, the modern man of today, the maze has become a matrix. My only hope to stay in touch with myself and with God is by deliberately choosing solitude. It's a choice I must defend against my culture, a culture lost to its complication, a culture that is hyper-aware of all that might happen but is seemingly ignorant of what will.

I often talk about the reality that everyone is created unique and how special we are that there's no one else like us. But in his book *Beloved*, Henri Nouwen pointed out that a consequence of our being unique is our aloneness: "There's nobody like you around," he said. That uniqueness creates "a kind of separateness . . . that we constantly struggle to overcome, because we feel our aloneness quickly becomes loneliness."

And that loneliness, said Nouwen, is "probably one of the greatest sufferings of our time." The only relief from it is God, who "wants all your attention and who wants to give you all the love you need."[7]

In successful solitude there is no one but you and God.

Letting God alone speak to me, being alone with God to love me, letting God alone comfort me—these choices are what "loving myself for God's sake" looks like. *In solitude I am not alone. I am alone with God.*

As Chesterton wrote, "It is only the Mystic, the man who accepts contradictions, who can laugh and walk easily through the world."[8]

Humbled by Mystery

If we live long enough, the conclusion that comes from knowledge is mystery. With enough confusing personal knowledge, we become mystics.

Now that I have enough failed experience, I am humbled by mystery. The result leaves me feeling a bit helpless and foolish but also a bit wiser and a bit more relaxed.

Later in life Thomas Aquinas was writing *The Sum of All Theology* when he encountered the glory of God—the mystery. After all his beautiful writings about God, his experience of this holy mystery left him speechless. He wrote nothing more and counted his previous words about God "as like straw."

I imagine he also felt a bit wiser and a bit more relaxed.

Before, I had more answers than faith. I now have more faith than answers.

Life has mystery, and paradox, and is miraculous. I agree with Albert Einstein when he said: "There are two ways to live your life. One is as if nothing is a miracle. The other is as if everything is."[9] Living your life as if everything is a miracle could also serve as a definition of *childlike*.

There's a great peace that comes from faith that trusts when it doesn't know, believes when it can't see, and loves because that is the nature of God's love.

All this living out of "not yet" is the confrontation that challenges everything about us, and in particular our faith in God. Being honest in our trials includes acknowledging our confusion and sometimes our doubts. God invites us to honestly struggle in our faith because our faith and our love in God are planted in these trials. Trusting, believing, and loving God in spite of all we face is living faith. He promises to always be with us, even when we don't see or understand. Even when we are confused. Even when we doubt.

God is always more than my knowledge or experience. Always. I should accept that and be wiser . . . and a bit more relaxed.

The sciences rarely create. Most of the time they only discover what they don't know.

Some things *are* mysteries; they just are.

I was watching a scientist as he explained, confidently and precisely, what happened sixty-five million years ago. And then, in a most sophisticated and credible voice, the narrator stated, "What has been a mystery for all time . . . is no longer."

I laughed out loud.

Somehow mankind hopes more knowledge will explain the mystery. The religious believe that heaven will reveal it. But I tend to imagine heaven to be not the end of mysteries but the beginning, where there are no secrets being kept, just mysteries waiting to be revealed.

The confusion of experience will often introduce mystery *as* revelation, and the pride of man will always try to explain the mystery away. But those efforts are childish and display ignorance as well as arrogance. As C. S. Lewis argued, "Can a mortal ask questions which God finds unanswerable? Quite easily, I should think, all nonsense questions are unanswerable. How many hours are in a mile? Is yellow square or round? Probably half the questions we ask—half our great theological and metaphysical problems—are like that."[10]

To "love myself for God's sake" is the freedom to accept I'm ignorant. I always was, only now I know it.

Choir Practice, 40″ x 30″

CONFUSED BY EXPERIENCE
AND SPARED SUCCESS

Doubts are the messengers of the Living One to the honest. They
are the first knock at our door of things that are not yet, but
have to be understood. . . . Doubt must precede every deeper
assurance; for uncertainties are what we first see when we look
into a region hitherto unknown, unexplored, unannexed.

—*George Macdonald in C.S. Lewis,* Anthology

Experience can be confusing, but it also offers the advantage of
looking back.

I had a friend who started a business. After two years of torment and struggle, he finally failed. A year later he said, "If I had
been a little more successful, I'd still be doing it."

If he had continued, he might still be tormented to this day.
Still slogging along, barely making it. Still consumed with failure.
But to finally admit failure or foolishness in our lives provides the
freedom to change.

The freedom God offers is to stop the torment and to change our struggle from what we have considered the good by picking up the best that God offers.

Are there things I struggle with in my life that torment *me*? Am I being just successful enough, strong enough, or stubborn enough to keep on doing them? How long have I carried on, not giving in to God by admitting my need or receiving His forgiveness? The thought makes me think of how often His merciful futility has brought me to a stop, defeated. Then to the place I start again, with God—forgiven and restored.

I have wanted so many successes that would have destroyed me.

God, I wasn't very thankful at the time, but looking back, I need to thank You for all the success You spared me.

What would You spare me today?

Looking back, I now see clearly—
how clearly I thought stupid thoughts.
Now, being older and with more experience,
I can't help but wonder . . .
what is stupid today?

There's a memorable line in the film *The Natural* that pierced my heart when I first heard it. "We have two lives," one of the characters says, "the life we learn with, and the life we live after that."

Beautiful and tragic, the words remind me of God's mercy. And of my life. And of my art. All my art has been practice work, art that I learned with. Even the paintings I sold—no, especially those. They were the best practice pieces.

I imagine today's life of faith is practice for tomorrow. But it won't be until tomorrow, with God, that I understand fully that today was only practice.

I've continued to think about the line from the film and have come to realize it's also what God's forgiveness has been like for me: a second chance for a life after sin. His forgiveness makes all things new . . . again.

As beautiful as it is, that movie line doesn't compare to the beauty of a God who has given me more than two lives, more than three. In fact, He makes *all* things new again, and again, and again.

God starts a new life for me every time I repent. That's one reason I like repenting—not just to get a new start, but also to keep my relationship with God unhindered by my sin.

Not a Test

It's easy to imagine this life as a test, but I don't see it so much as a test as it is an opportunity to know God. Besides, He said He'd do the test for me (if there were a test I had to pass). But many people approach this life, not as a relationship with God but as though there were a need to gain some degree or to attain some diploma. Or maybe a mere passing grade would do.

For those who insist life is a test, it must be multiple choice. They first go through their choices of A, B, C, and D, but none of those answers solves the problem. Sometimes it takes a lifetime to try all the choices. Then, at the end of life, fewer choices remain, and they are simpler: Do I choose all of the above or none of the above?

Do I choose God, or not choose God?

Bad Compositions Make Bad Foundations

It's not what I see that I paint. It's what I see that *inspires* what I paint.

What I see in life should inspire me to be creative. To creatively love. To creatively serve. To creatively give. And when I'm confused by what I see, God wants me to use my heart more than my eyes.

In the same way, He wants me to use His love more than mine in the painting of my life.

In art, it is better to paint a good painting than to try to make a bad painting good—because despite the artist's best efforts, a bad painting usually stays bad. Why? Usually because it's a bad composition, which really means the foundation was bad. Regardless of what gets built on top of it, that foundation stays bad from the ground up.

The foundations of my life in the previous stages have been selfishness without God, selfishness with God, and disappointed self-righteousness. This final foundation is built on God Himself. No other foundation will stand. You can paint well on canvas even when the foundation of the painting is bad, but your best efforts will be in vain.

The Master Artist looks to my foundations, regardless of how I try to cover over my flaws. Regardless of my fancy brushwork or veneer finishes, He sees.

Unconditional Faith

What if to find love—I first need to know God?

Just like the old rock 'n' roll song says, most of us are "lookin' for love in all the wrong places." We look for it in a spouse, in our children, our family and friends, even in religion, or creation, or social causes. The list is long, the search is wearisome, and peace eludes us until we find it.

We "find" love through the experience of contradiction and paradox: more in giving than in receiving, and yet we selfishly demand a love we don't want to offer. When we don't get that love we demand, we reject the idea altogether as fantasy. We may consider love as blind, but Chesterton argued, "Love is not blind; that is the last thing it is. Love is bound; and the more bound it is the less it is blind."[1]

We've looked everywhere for love except its Source. *God* is love. The love you've hoped for and dreamed of is no fantasy. God is not mad *at* you; He's mad *about* you. Regardless of who you have been or what you have done, His love is the gift you can give to others and still hold on to yourself. In His love our hearts find the rest we have searched for, longed for.

But before you can share it, you have to receive it.

I have come to understand the love of God through loving my children. They receive the closest thing I can express as my unconditional love. There were times when I couldn't imagine God loving me unconditionally, but when I thought of how I love my children, I could understand how He might.

Some people seem to talk with God in conversation. I guess I do too, but only a few times have I heard a clear voice in words I understood. One morning when my daughters were little, I was leaving early before anyone was up. I checked the girls and then came back into the bedroom and kissed Cath as she slept. I turned to leave and heard, *Love her like your children.* Then silence.

I stood there, not sure if I had imagined it, and then, knowing I hadn't, questioned, *What did He mean?*

In the next instant, I understood. I loved my children unconditionally but not my wife.

It would be nice to tell you that ever since that day I have loved Cath unconditionally. I have not. I have many different loves for Cath: as my wife, my friend, and sister. All with some conditions. But I love her best when I consider loving her with the love a father has for his child.

God offers us His unconditional love. Our response should be to love Him back with unconditional faith.

Hiding in a Crowd

Soren Kierkegaard said, "If you want to be loathsome to God, just run with the herd."[2] I think he might be right. God wants an intimate relationship with us. To deny Him intimacy by trying to hide in a group is far from His intent—even if the group is a religion, a church, or a spouse. He is a jealous God.

I can look back on my life and see the herds I hid in and how they defined me. I can see how protected I felt when I was in the center of such groups, whether they consisted of people or philosophies. I have traded less godly groups for more godly ones. But as my life runs out, I realize that I still struggle to be alone with God apart from my peers and my philosophies. Even my theologies are like fig leaves I cover myself with, because of my discomfort at being naked before God.

My desire to be individual comes from God. Before God, I must become me, myself, as I—and no one else.

For too much of my Christian life, I have enjoyed the company and thoughts of others more than I have enjoyed the company of God. I realize I have stayed busy much of my life to avoid being alone with Him. In doing so, I have denied His "still small voice"[3] as I huddle around other, louder voices that are more comforting and less threatening to my religion.

I Pledge Allegiance to . . . ?

There have been a great number of studies about peer pressure and its effects on human behavior. What's interesting to me is that we recognize peer pressure outside the church but not in the church. We imagine that our good intentions protect us from this herd mentality. We imagine that, because we love God, our cause must be just and our course must be true.

We don't admit to ourselves that we search out fellowships that agree with us.

C. S. Lewis was referring to our very strong and yet very insecure need to belong when he said, "Of all passions, the passion for the 'Inner Ring' is making a man who is not yet very bad do very bad things."[4] This insecurity drives us by our inner natures.

Oswald Chambers helped me understand with these words: "A person's inner nature, what he possesses in the inner, spiritual part of his being, determines what he is tempted by on the outside."[5]

Our desires to belong are decided by our dispositions, spiritual or otherwise. Sometimes our temptations are for what we consider the good, not the bad.

But to imagine that my desires for good are free from sin is only my imagination. Through some twisted logic, we may even excuse our actions, thinking we are doing bad things for good reasons.

What inner ring are *you* pining for? It may not be evil, but your desire for it may be. You may not lust to be a drug lord, but you might lust to be a deacon.

If we find a ring—a herd—to belong to, we soon become defenders of our ring. Proving our allegiance, we judge others who are not in our ring. And, as Pascal offered, they lead us to even more sinister places: "Men never do evil so completely and cheerfully as when they do it from religious conviction."[6]

Our challenge is this: Do we conform to the herd, or do we conform to God? Do we manage our image because we fear being cast out of our ring, or do we live honestly and transparently with those around us? Do we offer love freely and unconditionally, or do we give love in order to get love in return?

My own faith is often challenged and my courage tested on whether my allegiance is to God, and to God alone.

In solitude, and probably only there, will you hear Christ calling you out by name, calling you individually and not as a part of a group or as a member of an organization. Nouwen wrote that it was in the quiet of solitude that he could feel the tenderness of

God's love and hear God speak of His love for him. Likewise, in silent solitude we can hear God say, "You are my beloved." There we can answer as Nouwen did: "Yes, Lord, I love you too."[7]

This conversation, in solitude with God, might continue with some pointed questions and hard answers: "Are you worshiping an idol? Have you found your peace, hope, and joy in a herd and not in Me?"

Blinded by His Light

When I'm blinded by God's light, I may not see clearly, but He clearly sees me. As an artist, I prefer backlit scenes, finding them more beautiful. The light flows from behind, creating mysteries by outlining shapes and creating unnoticed patterns. Where there's strong contrast, the light can be so bright that most details are lost in it.

Driving your car, you can clearly see this for yourself. Driving into the sun, though it can be difficult and uncomfortable, makes the most mundane countryside take on a mysterious beauty. By comparison, if you travel with the light at your back, you can see more easily because everything is comfortably illuminated and understood.

For me, pursuing God seems similar. As I pursue Him, I am traveling toward the light, not away from it. I may feel uncomfortable because I can't see clearly; I may feel tempted to look away. My challenge is this: Will I continue when I'm blinded by His light? Will I move into mystery? Or will I prefer a mundane existence and stay where I am, sticking with what I understand?

Thomas T. Lynch wrote, "He that lives in shade does not see his own shadow; he that walks in sunshine does."[8] If we live in a "shadowland," we only imagine our godliness or our wickedness, but we can't see the fullness of either. It is also here that evil convinces us either to hold on to our shame or to hide it.

Without God's light there is no contrast and no seeing the truth about ourselves, other people, or even God Himself. But,

> if we walk in the light, as he is in the light, we have fellowship with one another, and the blood of Jesus, his Son, purifies us from all sin. If we claim to be without sin, we deceive ourselves and the truth is not in us. If we confess our sins, he is faithful and just and will forgive us our sins and purify us from all unrighteousness. If we claim we have not sinned, we make him out to be a liar, and his word is not in us.[9]

I do not see accurately except in the light of Christ. Unless I want the truth, I will stay in the shadows and only imagine the heights of my good and the depths of my bad.

The Scots have a wise old saying: "When you measure yer shadow, do it wi' a high sun." It must have been noon, with the bright light of Christ shining down on him, when the apostle Paul "measured his shadow" and wrote that he was "chief" of sinners.[10] To see his sin so clearly, he must have been standing very close to God.

I imagine that if we were to approach God—and get close enough—we would think the same about our own shadows. We might even challenge Paul's claim to be the chief.

With God encouraging us, we need not despair because with His help we see ourselves being changed into the likeness of His Son, and the shadow we cast taking Christ's form. Seeing who I really am in God's light is a mercy, not a curse; a hope, not despair. If I choose to live in this "shadowland," I may make myself king of my fantasy world, but nevertheless I reign in darkness.

The Shadows We Cast

There is one more aspect to this "shadow talk," and that's the reality that we *do* cast shadows. As Anna E. Hamilton wrote,

> *This I learned from the shadow of a tree,*
> *That to and fro did sway upon a wall:*
> *Our shadow-selves, our influence, may fall*
> *Where we can never be.*[11]

The shadow we cast is seen and felt by others, some near, some far, and some yet to come. The influence we cast depends on who we are. Not just what others may see but who we are before God in private. More often than not, we are unconscious and unaware of who is being touched by our real shadow.

Are our shadows of Christ or of something less? When people are touched by *your* shadow, what impact does it have? What do they feel? Love and mercy—or hypocrisy and judgment?

People like to talk about legacy, but legacy is usually a conscious effort to create a positive memory of ourselves before we die, a way we try to increase our own pleasure or our own stature—too often, shrines to our reign on earth.

The godliest people who influenced me would rarely have considered themselves worthy of such credit. They probably didn't worry about a legacy; they were too busy living the moments of their lives with God. They didn't know how blessed I was by their lives touching mine because they were unconscious of their shadows, shadows that outlined the image of Christ wherever they turned, casting shades of blessings wherever they went.

Life for Death

In life, our knowledge about someone is a confusion, full of contradictions, a paradox of good and bad.

In death, the memory of someone is a changeling: if he or she were a good person, we seem to forget his or her bad, and if he or she were bad, we can't seem to remember the good.

To consider my imminent death should make me lucid, not morbid. I hope when I face death that I don't model it poorly, that I don't suffer doubt and fear, and that I have my best days of faith as I die.

I hope. I pray.

But still, death is a problem for me, because I'm torn between the road and the water, between the earth I know and the heaven I hope for. Dave Crowder stated the problem for us all: "Everybody wants to go to heaven, but nobody wants to die."[12]

I hope to have eager anticipation, as the deaf composer Beethoven reportedly did, exclaiming on his deathbed, "I shall hear in heaven!" Of course he will.

Even the least spiritual person recognizes that this physical life ends. So why is it, if I believe in God and the hope of heaven, that I would pray more about the healing of the cancer in my body than the cancer in my soul?

If faith is a basis for healing, when is it not a lack of faith to die? When would it be a lack of faith not to want to die?

In the Depths of His Peace

A peace has started to form deep in my heart, out of sight, at the depths of my foundations. The peace is God Himself and His love for me as I love myself for His sake.

He has been faithful to me, and I realize my greatest doubts were about *me, my* faith, *my* religion, and *my* god. Not so much about Him.

Without being able to completely explain it, I believe God will make me whole and holy the day I die. And I feel certain that God answers all our good prayers but sometimes with answers we don't always want.

I have peace . . . His. And I have joy, because I want God more than I want what I want.

Perfect Day, 10″ x 8″

12

WHERE THE ROAD
TURNS TO WATER

We can flee evil either out of fear for punishment—
like slaves, or, out of hope for reward—like hirelings,
or, out of love for God—like children.

—*Soren Kierkegaard*, Provocations

It's the love of God that sets me free, but it's believing He loves me
that sets me free to love others.

In his book *The Man Who Was Thursday*, G. K. Chesterton
closes with his characters dressing up. In this allegory, they all come
to find that their new outfits "did not disguise, but reveal."[1]

I have worn many disguises, most of my own making and
most to hide weaknesses and failures. Now, in this stage of loving
myself for God's sake, God is asking me to put on what feels like
a disguise—a robe of His righteousness.

At first I refuse. It's unbelievable, yet His love and His will are
clear. I put it on. At first it feels awkward and ill-fitting. Worse, it

feels like a lie. But then I discover there's something true about this costume; it's surprisingly comfortable and comfortingly real. As it rests on my shoulders, I wonder, *Is this what I am becoming, or a forgotten memory of what I once was?*

Then, remembering Paul's words to the Colossians, I understand what I'm wearing:

> You must clothe yourselves with tenderhearted mercy, kindness, humility, gentleness, and patience. . . . And the most important piece of clothing you must wear is love.[2]

Jesus began a prayer for you and me. It began on the cross. It continues in heaven. And it starts with these words: "Father, forgive them, for they know not what they do."

Grace and Redemption

In an art composition, the light and dark values are divided into positive and negative spaces, each defining the other and sharing their boundaries.

In life, knowledge and mystery are parts of the same composition, each defining the other, and sharing their boundaries. They are parts of the same whole, sharing the same space. Good questions don't always lead to good answers. They might only silhouette the shapes of mystery and outlines of grace.

The mystery of my fickle heart has broad outlines of grace. Who am I? By the grace of God I am His. And when I look deepest into this heart of mine, I see the outlines of grace defining the mystery of my redemption.

What lies deepest within me is not sin but God.

Our real test is always with God alone and no one else to help or hinder us. Our truest tests come when no one else would know, and yet, we still choose God. Still surrender to Him. Still love and forgive. Whether anyone but God Himself will ever know.

I pray, when you are free to do as you please, that you look deep within yourself and there see the outlines of grace forming a silhouette of Christ.

To Love Like God

In his book *Mortal Lessons*, Dr. Richard Selzer tells a beautiful story about the love between a young married couple. To surgically remove a tumor, a facial nerve had to be cut in the wife's beautiful face, which resulted in a wry smile that drooped to one side.

After the surgery, the husband entered the room and understood that her face would remain as he saw it. Selzer shares what happened next when he could not escape the intimacy of their moment. The husband smiled reassuringly and said, "I like it; it's kind of cute."

He continues:

All at once I know who he is. I understand and lower
my gaze. One is not bold in an encounter with a god.
Unmindful, he bends down to kiss her crooked mouth
and I am so close I can see how he twists his own lips
to accommodate hers, to show that their kiss still works.

I still cry when I read this, for its beauty and its love. But
there's another reason I cry. Because just like the husband in this
scene, I think of you God, and how You have bent down to kiss
my twisted mouth, and how you twist your own lips to kiss mine
that are so twisted.

Tears of disbelief flow as You reassure me that our kiss still
works . . . in spite of my sin. And that You still call me beloved, and
tell me I am beautiful.

Who are You, God? What kind of God are you that would love
me like this, when I feel so ugly?[3]

When Jesus asked Peter, "Are you leaving me too?" Peter
answered, "Lord, I have no place else to go." If Jesus were to ask
me that question at this point in my life, I might answer, "Lord, I
have no place left to go."[4]

The Greatest Paradox

After all these experiences with God, I still struggle with the greatest paradox of all—myself. I am fearfully and wonderfully made,
in His image, yet fearfully original and wonderfully unique. I now
see that I fashioned most of my doubt and confusion out of my
own surplus stockpiles of conceit and disappointment. There was
actually very little about God in those fears.

At this stage of the journey, I am becoming convinced that God has a plan for me that stretches beyond this life. Something that requires me to have more faith because there's no way I could understand the fullness of God's desire. Ignorance isn't stupid; it's just ignorant. But we get stupid fast when we insist on knowing things. To trust and obey isn't *too* simple; it's simple enough.

I was created on purpose, for a purpose. My original design and unique creation are being rescued by God, not melted down. I am not so much losing my identity as I am being lovingly refined.

As we approach God, we don't become more alike, but less alike. We are alike only as originals. What we share is uniqueness.

In Romans 8, Paul described the pains of this life as a pregnant condition and, by application, he likened the pains of giving birth to the life of God in *my* life:

> These sterile and barren bodies of ours are yearning for full deliverance. That is why waiting does not diminish us, any more than waiting diminishes a pregnant mother.[5]

God is here to help me along and knows my pregnant condition. By His Spirit, He prays for and through me. By His love, He comforts me and knows me better than I know myself. There is nothing that can separate His love from me. Nothing. That's His promise, not mine.

Whether birthing circumstance, consequence, or poem—with every thought, word, and action, I create. Loving and forgiving are the highest art forms I create in; they're the most Godlike.

Salvation Is Birthed

I wasn't interested in a relationship with God when I started this journey; it was all about me. Later it was still about me but with a new label and a recommitment of my pride. I still wasn't interested in the relationship part, except the part where God blessed me. Sadly, even now, I see this is still too much about me.

In the first three stages, it was up to me to pretend and to perform, and learn. Now, with my own confused experience behind me, I know it isn't how I look, it isn't what I do, and it isn't what I know that matters. What's most important is my relationship with my Redeemer, the Lover of my soul.

There is a great difference between the knowledge of God and a relationship with Him. Knowing about something is not knowing *Someone*. And with God, it's only the relationship that counts, because knowledge of God doesn't require any relationship at all.

Salvation is not birthed without relationship, even when you believe the right stuff.

Freedom to Trust

I finished my coffee and got the check, no hurry. The flight was on time, the gate in sight, as I watched a three-year-old lead his father on an expedition.

Confident, he took off, turning left, then right, looking up, then down, totally self-centered as passengers parted to accommodate the path he was creating.

This independence, this freedom—was the child rebelling?

The toddler's father shadowed his every move. Dad made sure everyone noticed the little explorer as they moved out of his way.

The child charged onward, seemingly unaware of his parent's alert protection.

But then I saw the boy look back. Just a glance. And then he continued, looked back again, and hurried on, repeatedly casting childish eyes backward, carelessly confirming Dad's presence in his wake.

I now understood: he was aware, certain, and reassured that his daddy was right behind him. If he had looked back and didn't see him, the joyful expedition would have abruptly ended and immediate terror would have begun.

How much of our lives are we free to explore, invited to explore, because of our Father's constant presence? How aware are we of the comfort we feel knowing He is right behind us? How reassured, knowing He is watching out for us? How alert, as we charge carelessly ahead in the freedom of His care? And how mindful are we now of all those foolish times when we fought God, when He was only picking us up so we wouldn't be hurt or lost?

Thinking of the airport toddler, I understand that this independence and freedom is not always rebellion; it can also be trust:

> Relish your youthful vigor.
> Follow the impulses of your heart.
> If something looks good to you, pursue it.

But know also that not just anything goes;
You have to answer to God for every last bit of it.[6]

My Path That Is His

We all have our own paths, paths that lead us to God or away from Him. My most direct path to God is from where I am, not from where I'm not. It's not someone else's path; it's *my* path. I have a road that is His.

If I turn to God, immediately my path narrows, and I leave a broad road with many people. If I stay on the path, it will continue to narrow. Sometimes I am surprised by where it is leading, but I will follow Him wherever He leads.

There isn't just one narrow path to God . . . it's that He guides me on my narrow path to Him.

When I allow Him to be my Guide and Shepherd, I have no want. He leads me beside still waters on sunny days and takes my hand as we walk together through the dark nights. He comforts my fears and leads me to our home, where His love will chase after me all the days of my forever.

Sometimes in the dark, I've come so close to Him that the only voice I hear is His.

Sometimes in the light, He's so close I can no longer see the path ahead. Still I follow.

I walk my path that is His, knowing He is leading me home, to the home He has prepared for me.

Jesus said, "Don't let your heart be troubled. You trust Me, don't you? There's plenty of room in My Father's house. I'm leaving to prepare a place for you. I will come back for you and take you to live where I live . . . You know the road I am taking."

But, Lord, I don't know where You're going. How do You expect me to know the road?

Jesus answered, "I am the road, and the truth, and the life."[7]

To live in this stage of loving myself for God's sake is to freely live in God's grace, *willfully* becoming the object of His ransoming love. Willfully becoming who God created me to be—and no one else.

Through the stages of this life I have tried to "get" God, but now, in surrender, I ask God to come and get me.

At the End of the Road, an Eternal Revelation

Nearing the end of this road, I am excited to find my deepest desires are for God, and I am genuinely surprised by how much love I feel for God and others. There is no completion to this life, or the next. If it's healthy, it's continually growing, changing, and evolving.

My relationship with God, and I imagine with heaven as well, will be an eternal revelation of a continuous and glorious completing where God sets me free to be who I was always intended to be. And to discover the truth: that He has always loved me. Who I *am*. I don't need to fear that I must become someone or something other than myself, something different than His original creation of me, or of you. This creating has only begun. Eternally, He will continue the glorious redemption of our relationships.

Now, at the end of my journey, walking along the water with a limp, wounded by God's love, I can finally see that where the road turns to water is where the road turns to love. Love that embraces, completes, and is heaven itself.

> *Faith that is only religion is too fragile, too fussy, and too demanding to become real faith.*

When are we who we were intended to be? Nearer the endings than the beginnings of things—

The endings of my wisdom, my mercy, my love, and the beginnings of God's wisdom, mercy, and love, birthed in my heart.

Sometimes it does take a long time, but God is patient.

Sometimes hurts and regrets leave me broken, but He is merciful.

Sometimes I even betrayed His love, but He is forgiving.

He still calls me to beauty, and He still calls me beautiful. He offers me His love to make me His.

"Where the Road Turns to Water" is where the

beginnings of the endings are, where not yets are met, and what could be . . . is.

Only Your merciful love has prevailed, Lord. Only Your forgiving love has truly seen. I worship and adore You . . . my tears reaching the water.

A Fourth Prayer

Our Father who art in heaven, hallowed be Thy name.
I worship You.

Thy kingdom come; Thy will be done on earth as it is in heaven.
As You say.

Give us this day our daily bread.
Thank You.

Forgive us our trespasses as we forgive those who trespass against us.
I will forgive.

And lead me not into temptation, but deliver me from evil.
You are my refuge.

Yours is the kingdom, and the power, and the glory forever, Lord.
And forever. Amen.

The Endings of Beginnings

This poem-prayer is for those of us who have been confused in this
pursuit of God, and whose desire is to know, love, and serve Him:

> After all my efforts, God doesn't love me more.
> After all my failures, God doesn't love me less.
> After all my frustration, He offers peace.
>
> After all my sin, He offers forgiveness.
> After all my shame, He offers hope.
> After all my attempts to be "someone better,"
> I realize He has called me to be who I am,
> Forgiven and loved, just as I am.
>
> His most important promise to me?
> The promise that He will finish what He started in me—
> He offers His Love, even though
> I have refused to be broken in order to appear whole.
> Refused to be weak to appear strong.
> Refused His wisdom to appear wise.
> Refused to be humble to appear confident.
> I have even refused to love to appear holy.
> Forgive me.
> Lord, help me.
> I know that until I give up trying to be good,
>   pretending to be someone, or something I'm not.
> Until I surrender,

accepting God's love and forgiveness
wherever and whoever I am.
Until that happens, I don't have You, I only have religion,
a faith of legalism that breeds lovelessness.

A religiousness that gives me doctrines to judge others by
and beliefs that leave me strangled by guilt and shame.
All the while,
You wait for me to give up my religious ways
and all my failed attempts to be holy.

"God, help me." I still think this is about me!
I lay down my illusions of control
but also understand You will not take my free will.
I must choose, and I choose You.
I have seen Your grace—
Misrepresented by the church as something earned.
Misrepresented by the world as something weak.
And I have misrepresented Your love when I haven't offered
the same love You've given me.
Not for fear of punishment, or hope for reward, but for love.
I will put my faith in You,
To stay broken, filled with Your Joy. To become so weak,
You're my only hope.
To rest in Your love, freely loving others.
And finding my deepest true desire is to love God and man,
unconditionally and without limitation. It's all about You,
God, and what You did for me.
You did it all; You did everything.

What is left for me to do?
To humbly accept what You've done,
    trust what You're doing, and love who You are.
That's it—that's the secret.

Now with God's own love, we can offer one another,
Deepest thanks and deeper apologies.

I offer a prayer for myself—and maybe for you if you're sharing my journey:

God,
You are so much more merciful than I could have ever imagined in my youth. My life, my need for You, has been beyond my reason—my need for Your love beyond my logic, my need for Your faithfulness profound in my unfaithfulness.

Somehow, I completely underestimated Your grace. I received it but underestimated my need of it. I believed it but underestimated the power of it.

And wanting it, I'm shocked how fierce Your love can be; it *is* scandalous.

Deepest thanks for Your merciful patience, endless grace, and undeserved love.

And deeper apologies that it's taken a lifetime of Your forgiveness to convince me of Your love.

Amen and amen.

Majesty, 16″ x 12″

EPILOGUE:
ARRIVING ON THE SHORE
OF HEAVEN AND EARTH

How often do we look upon God as our last and feeblest
resource? We go to Him because we have nowhere else to
go. And then we learn that the storms of life have driven
us, not upon the rocks, but into the desired haven.

—George MacDonald,
Annals of a Quiet Neighborhood

This long road has been a journey through stages, and even when I love myself for God's sake, it's difficult to stay here because, for now, sin is a part of creation and a part of me. The gravitational pull of my selfishness is so strong that I know it's impossible for me to overcome without God's help.

This road has led to "where the road turns to water." It has ended on the shore between heaven and earth, the place where the physical and the spiritual touch. The place where the physical world begins to fade away, where you can almost hear heaven.

I imagine this shore is the final destination. But the road I have traveled still remains. Even though I stand on the shore, having come so far, I can still turn and go back if I choose.

Throughout these experiences I have been proud and deceived as well as broken and humbled. I battled my greatest foe—my *self*. I found evil to be more frightening than powerful, and I was confused and enlightened in the very same moment. I have been found guilty, pardoned by God Himself, and given beauty for my ashes.

Finally, *my* road has turned to water where it has met God's heavenly shore.

My hope and prayer for us all is to arrive and stay on that shore until the day we see Him coming for us . . . walking on the water.

GRATITUDES

The road has been long and this page is too short to explain the miracles of God involved, not just in this book, but in every aspect of my life that created the book. So, for now, I will offer this too brief thanks to the too few:

To God first, for Your patience and tender mercy to me, especially when I was discouraged and whining.

To Cath, not just for all you have been to me, but for all you bring to my life and our family. You are beautiful—and good looking too.

I thank God for you, my children, and my children's children. This great love I have for you is but God Himself. You help me see God.

To my parents for your constant love and encouragement. I miss you, Pop. For me, you modeled unconditional love.

To all those who have molded my life for God as teachers, friends, and fellow strugglers, I am eternally grateful.

To the many men's groups over the years, and particularly for my current Monday and Wednesday guys. These past years I have been blessed by the presence of God in your lives. Your friendship holds me and keeps me on the Way.

To my friends Bill and Sharon Carlson, who introduced me to my agent, Sealy Yates, and finally, to Worthy Publishing, where everyone—but in particular, Rob Birkhead and Kris Bearss—encouraged, helped, and gifted their patience to the novice and all his fragile feelings. Thank you.

I also had the blessing, and the need, to work with two other editors. (I think they both were trying to fast track my sketchy talents with English and grammar.) The first major rewrite came with Ken Gire. Ken, you were a blessing from God, a wise counselor, and a good friend to me. Thank you. Next came Sue Ann Jones, who showed me even more of what I couldn't see myself. Again, wise, encouraging, and educational. Thank you for your patience and guidance.

I appreciated it all, and I learned so much from all you pros—especially the lessons in kindness and humility.

And to the many author saints, past and present, who shared their lives, inspiring mine on toward God: thank you for your courage, and I thank God for your words and lives.

To my family and friends, I love you. Words cannot express my gratitude or love. Thank you. And God bless you, one and all.

NOTES

A Note of Explanation
1. G. K. Chesterton, *William Blake* (New York: E. P. Dutton, 1920), 131.

Introduction: The Colors on God's Palette
1. C. S. Lewis, *A Grief Observed* (London: Faber, 1961. Reprinted with foreword by Madeleine L'Engle. San Francisco: Harper & Row, 1989), 88.
2. Pierre Teilhard De Chardin, *Pierre Teilhard De Chardin Writings*, with an introduction by Ursula King (Maryknoll, NY: Orbis Books, 1999).
3. St. Bernard of Clairvaux, *On the Love of God and Other Selected Writings*, ed. Charles J. Dollen (New York: AlbaHouse, 1996), 19–24.
4. A. W. Tozer, *Signposts: A Collection of Sayings from A. W. Tozer* (Wheaton, IL: Victor Books, 1964), 57.

Chapter 2: Selfishly Deceived and Hopelessly Proud
1. Nicholas of Cusa, *The Vision of God*, trans. Emma G. Salter (New York: E. P. Dutton, 1928), 76.
2. Tozer, *Signposts*, 103.
3. C. S. Lewis, *The Quotable Lewis* (Carol Stream, IL: Tyndale House, 1990), 496.

Chapter 3: Imagining Our Strength and Others' Weakness
1. Widely attributed to Plato, classical Greek philosopher.
2. See Matthew 5:43-48.
3. Galatians 6:9, 2 Thessalonians 3:13 KJV.
4. Galatians 6:1–5, personalized.
5. Brennan Manning, *Ragamuffin Gospel Visual Edition: Good News for the Bedraggled, Beat-Up, and Burnt Out* (Colorado Springs: Multnomah, 2005), 10.
6. Matthew 5:3–12.

Chapter 4: The Good Fortune of a Good God to Help Me on My Journey
1. Galatians 3:2–3 NIV.
2. Timothy Keller, *The Prodigal God* (New York: Dutton/Penguin Group, 2008), 44.
3. Romans 7:18–25, personalized.

Chapter 5: The Appearance of Evil—or Good
1. John Ruskin, quoted in L. B. Cowman, *Streams in the Desert* (Grand Rapids: Zondervan, 2006), 33.
2. Galatians 5:6, personalized.
3. Francis Schaeffer, *How Should We Then Live?* (Wheaton, IL: Crossway Books, 2005), 19.
4. Oswald Chambers, *My Utmost for His Highest* (1935; repr., Uhrichsville, OH: Barbour, 2000), August 29.
5. Oswald Chambers, *He Shall Glorify Me* (Fort Washington, PA: Christian Literature Crusade,1946), 585.
6. Manning, *Ragamuffin Gospel*, 7.
7. Source unknown.

Chapter 6: Refusing Mystery and Creating Fantasy Faith

1. 1 Peter 4:8 NLT.

2. See John 10:25, 30.

3. See St. Teresa of Avila, *The Autobiograhy of St. Teresa of Avila: The Life of St. Teresa of Jesus* (Rockford, IL: TAN Books and Publishers, 2009), 103.

Chapter 7: The Confusion of Having a Holy God Who Loves Me

1. Watchman Nee, *Sit, Walk, Stand* (Carol Stream, IL: Tyndale House, 1977).

2. Henri Nouwen with Philip Roderick, *Beloved: Henri Nouwen in Conversation* (Grand Rapids: Eerdmans, 2007), 30.

3. Elbert Hubbard, *Little Journeys to the Homes of Eminent Artists* (East Aurora, NY: Roycrofters Shop, 1912), 23.

Chapter 8: What Is Wrong with the World? We Are.

1. The story of Chesterton's newspaper editorial reply to the question, "What is wrong with the world?" has been widely reported, though the exact date of the original article is elusive. Chesterton elaborated on his answer in his book *What's Wrong with the World?* (Leipzig, Germany: Bernhard Tauchnitz, 1910). The book has been reprinted many times.

2. 1 Samuel 15:22 NCV.

3. G. K. Chesterton, *The Everlasting Man* (Peabody, MA: Hendrickson, 2007), 28.

4. Frederick Buechner, *Whistling in the Dark: A Doubter's Dictionary* (San Francisco: HarperCollins, 1993).

5. Nee, *Sit, Walk, Stand*.

Chapter 9: Loving Myself as My Neighbor

1. Henry Van Dyke, quoted on The Quotations Page, accessed August 15, 2011, http://www.quotationspage.com/quotes/Henry_Van_Dyke/.

2. George MacDonald, quoted in J E., *A Garland of Quiet Thoughts* (London: Simkin, Marshall, Hamilton, Kent, 1905), 68.

3. 2 Corinthians 12:9 NIV.

4. This Peter Cook quip appears on a coffee mug the author was given.

5. William Faulkner, quoted in Eugene Peterson, *A Long Obedience in the Same Direction* (Downers Grove, IL: InterVarsity Press, 1980), 22.

6. See Chambers, *My Utmost for His Highest*, September 27.

Chapter 10: Receiving God's Forgiveness and Love

1. Helen H. Lemmel, "Turn Your Eyes Upon Jesus," 1922.

2. Micah 6:8, author's paraphrase.

3. *The Book of Common Prayer*, 1979 (New York: Church Hymnal Corp, 2001), 360.

4. See Proverbs 18:24.

5. See Matthew 5:44 and Matthew 7:12.

6. Charles Wagner, *The Simple Life* (London: McClure, Phillips, 1901), 3.

7. Nouwen, *Beloved*, 5-9.

8. G. K. Chesterton, *Orthodoxy* (Garden City, NY: Image Books, 1959), 25.

9. Albert Einstein, quoted in *Journal of France and Germany* (1942–1944) by Gilbert Fowler White, in excerpt published in Robert E. Hinshaw, *Living with Nature's Extremes: The Life of Gilbert Fowler White* (Boulder, CO: Johnson Books, 2006), 62.

10. Lewis, *The Quotable Lewis*, 505.

Chapter 11: Confused by Experience and Spared Success

1. Chesterton, *Orthodoxy*, 76.
2. Soren Kierkegaard, quoted in Charles E. Moore, compiler, *Provocations—Spiritual Writings of Kierkegaard* (Rifton, NY: Plough, 1999), 244.
3. 1 Kings 19:12 KJV.
4. C. S. Lewis, *A Year with C. S. Lewis*, ed. Patricia S. Klein (San Francisco: Harper, 2003), 383.
5. Chambers, *My Utmost for His Highest*, September 17.
6. Blaise Pascal, *Pensees* (New York: Dutton, 1958), 86.
7. Nouwen, *Beloved*, 40.
8. Thomas T. Lynch, quoted in *The Evangelical Magazine and Missionary Chronicle* 3 (January 1861): 739.
9. 1 John 1:7–10 NIV.
10. See 1 Timothy 1:15 KJV.
11. Anna E. Hamilton, quoted in *Garland of Quiet Thoughts*, 65.
12. David Crowder and Mike Hogan wrote a book using this statement as the title: *Everybody Wants to Go to Heaven, But Nobody Wants to Die* (Grand Rapids: Zondervan, 2009).

Chapter 12: Where the Road Turns to Water

1. G. K. Chesterton, *The Man Who Was Thursday* (New York: Random House, 2001), 173.
2. Colossians 3:12, 14, author's paraphrase.
3. Richard Selzer, *Mortal Lessons* (New York: Simon and Schuster, 1976), 46.
4. See John 6:60–70.
5. Romans 8:23–25.
6. Ecclesiastes 11:9.
7. John 14:1–6, personalized.

Illustration images can be seen in full color at www.shortridgefineart.com.

Stephen Shortridge has been a professional artist for more than thirty years. In the 1970s and '80s he had a successful career in acting that included film, TV and commercials. In 1989 he left Los Angeles and acting to pursue his love of art. He has since become a world-renowned painter. His creativity and profound spiritual insights are reflected in both his painting and his writing. Stephen and his wife, Cathy, live in Coeur d'Alene, Idaho, where they raised their family and where they own The Painter's Chair Fine Art Gallery.

A complete biography and more information about Stephen's art is available at www.shortridgefineart.com.

WORTHY
P U B L I S H I N G

IF YOU LIKED THIS BOOK . . .

- Tell your friends by going to: http://deepest-thanks -deeper-apologies.com and clicking "LIKE"

- Share the video book trailer by posting it on your Facebook page

- Head over to our Facebook page, click "LIKE" and post a comment regarding what you enjoyed about the book

- Tweet "I recommend reading #DeepestThanksDeeper Apologies by Stephen Shortridge @Worthypub"

- Hashtag: #DeepestThanks

- Subscribe to our newsletter by going to http://worthy publishing.com/about/subscribe.php

WORTHY PUBLISHING
FACEBOOK PAGE

WORTHY PUBLISHING
WEBSITE

CPSIA information can be obtained at www.ICGtesting.com
Printed in the USA
LVOW07s0219041215

465312LV00016B/106/P